THE
TRANSKEIAN NATIVE TERRITORIES:
HISTORICAL RECORDS.

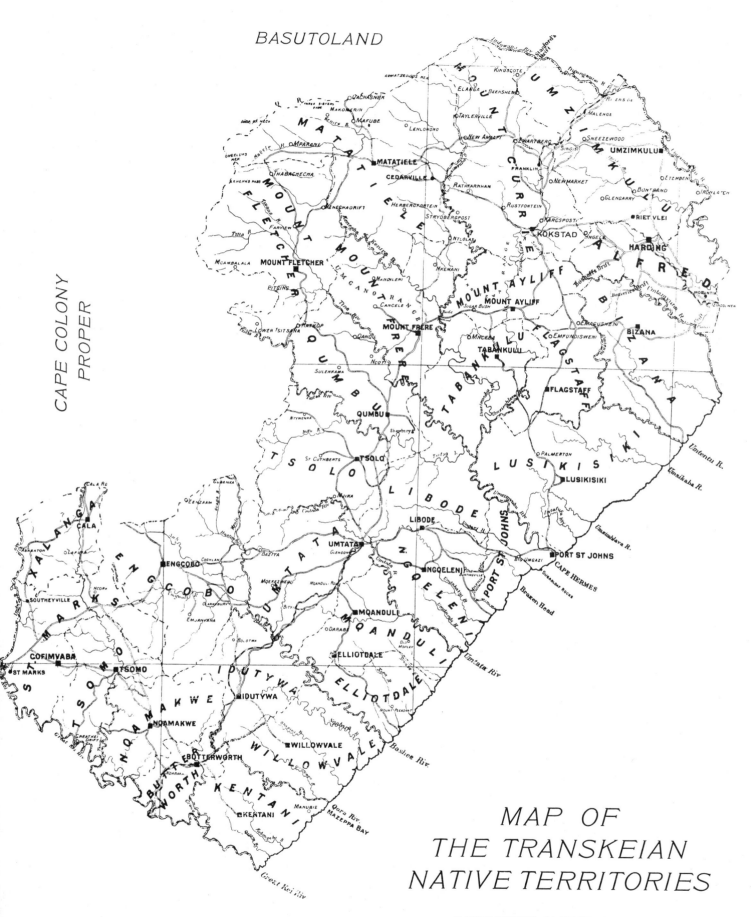

MAP OF
THE TRANSKEIAN
NATIVE TERRITORIES

*INCLUDING ALFRED COUNTY
IN NATAL.

THE

TRANSKEIAN NATIVE TERRITORIES:

HISTORICAL RECORDS

COMPILED BY

FRANK BROWNLEE,

RESIDENT MAGISTRATE, MOUNT AYLIFF,

EAST GRIQUALAND, S. A.

NEGRO UNIVERSITIES PRESS
WESTPORT, CONNECTICUT

Originally published in 1923
by Lovedale Institution Press

Reprinted from an original copy in the collections of
the Harvard College Library

Reprinted in 1970 by
Negro Universities Press
A Division of Greenwood Press, Inc.
Westport, Connecticut

Library of Congress Catalogue Card Number 75-129942

SBN 8371-1611-2

Printed in the United States of America

PREFATORY NOTE.

The object of this publication is to bring into handy form and to place within easy reach of those interested historical records which are not readily accessible to the General Public.

The records reproduced have not been tampered with except that a few obvious errors in the spelling of Native names, tribes and places have been amended. Portions of reports which have been considered superfluous have been deleted: mainly for this reason, several of the records in the appendix may appear to be bald, abrupt and without connection. The reproduction of these *in extenso* would have meant the inclusion of much non-essential matter.

The "Historical Sketch of the tribes anciently inhabiting Natal" has been included as the history of those tribes bore very directly upon the destinies of the Native people of the Transkeian Territories.

Mr. Orpen's memorandum deals principally with the tribes occupying the District of Mount Fletcher, in regard to whom only cursory reference has been made elsewhere.

*   *   *

The records take us up to about the year 1884 since when there have been many changes. The Administrative Policy which by that time had been laid upon a sound basis has been carried on by a younger generation of officials who have had before them as a guide the traditions and example of those who bore the heat and burden of the day "in dangers often."

The earlier officials by their patience, perseverance and fortitude made good in upholding the prestige of British Sovereignty. Through them the name and person of Queen Victoria came to be revered as they had come to be revered by all aboriginal tribes within the British Dominions as the final arbiter in any matters where white and coloured peoples might happen to be in juxtaposition and where any real or imagined grievance might seem to need adjustment.

The latter day official has not been faced with the physical dangers and difficulties which had to be met by those who went before but has to deal with a complexity of problems—social, economic, political, —coincident with the conditions of a people but lately emerged from barbarism and now progressing in civilisation and awakening to race-consciousness. The administration of the benevolent autocrat, which was entirely in accord with the Native form of government has given place to a system under which the executive officer is so hampered by rules, regulations and officialdom and his actions are so circumscribed as to allow of but little scope for imagination without which Native administration is greatly enfeebled. Meantime with the growth of initiative and individualism the Native is breaking away from the old order of things. A limit has been placed upon the despotic control of his chiefs, educational facilities have been brought within his reach, coupled with the beneficent influence of missionaries, consequently he is realising a sense of personal responsibility and is showing a growing capacity for achievement in the higher standards of civilisation.

Comparing the turbulent times of the "seventies" and early "eighties" with the present day placidity which has resulted from a wise, sympathetic and efficient administration aided by missionary co-operation, the Transkeian official cannot but feel a deep sense of the responsibility he has undertaken to build upon the great foundations laid by his predecessors.

*   *   *

Subsequent to the date to which these records bring us many events have occurred and a number of legislative measures have been introduced which have had far-reaching effects upon the destinies of the people. Among these may be mentioned the inauguration, extension and development of the Council System, the application of a code of penal laws, the annexation of Pondoland and outbreaks of Rinderpest and of East Coast Fever.

A great stride in advancement has been made with the introduction of the Council System which had its beginning as far back as 1882 in the "Fingoland District Fund" to which reference is made in the chapter on the Transkei.

Under the present system, provision is made for "District Councils for the administration of local affairs within the District." Each District Council consists of six Native members—four elected by the people and two nominated by the Magistrate. The Magistrate presides at the District Council meetings which are held quarterly.

Individual tenure of land as opposed to tribal or communal tenure is provided for, an arrangement by which each Native resident in a District may be enabled to acquire title to a residential and an arable allotment.

Once a year each District Council elects two and the Magistrate nominates one Native member to represent the District Council upon a General Council for the ensuing twelve months. The General Council meets once a year and is presided over by the Chief Magistrate. Magistrates of the Districts attend the General Council and have the right to take part in debate but have no vote.

The constitution of the General Council provides for the levy of a Rate of not less than 10/- per annum on each Native male resident within the area of its jurisdiction. The area of jurisdiction of the Transkeian Territories General Council includes eighteen Districts. The annual session is hed at Umtata. The Pondoland General Council includes the three Districts of Western Pondoland and sits at Libode.

The revenue derived from the Council Rate of 10/- is applied *inter alia* to the payment of the salaries of council officials, of authorised allowances to District and General Council members, the construction and maintenance of roads, bridges, cattle and sheep tanks and dams, the cost of plantations, establishing and maintaining industrial and agricultural schools and providing generally for the educational requirements of the people.

In 1886 a code of criminal law drawn up by the Commission on Native Laws and Customs of 1883, was put in force. The provisions of this code, which is entitled "The Transkeian Territories Penal Code," are based upon the terms of the Criminal Code of India. In drafting the code, full consideration was given to local conditions and requirements. For example the Native custom connected with spoor law was embodied in it. Under this custom where the spoor of lost stock is traced to the neighbourhood of a kraal, the head of that kraal is held liable for the value of the missing stock unless he is able to trace the spoor away from his kraal. Penalties are provided for persons practising witchcraft and for persons imputing to others the use of non-natural agencies. In short, the code contemplates every probable or possible common law offence that may occur in the conditions under which the people live. It has stood the test of time, such few statutory amendments as have been made having been of a minor nature.

Under the present judicial system, Magistrate's Courts deal with criminal charges of a minor nature. More important cases are heard before a Circuit Court consisting of a Judge and Jury sitting at specified centres twice a year.

In civil matters the Magistrate's jurisdiction is practically unlimited From his judgment an appeal lies (a) to the Supreme Court where one or both parties to the suit are Europeans; (b) to the Native Appeal Court where both parties are Natives.

The Native Appeal Court is presided over by the Chief Magistrate sitting with two Magistrates as Assessors and with Native Assessors who are consulted in cases where questions of Native custom may be at issue. It is an itinerant Court sitting periodically at specified centres.

*　　　　　*　　　　　*

The Chief Magistrate, who is the Chief Executive Officer of the Transkeian Territories, is responsible for the general administration of the Territories. He is the medium between Magistrates and the Secretary for Native Affairs and upon him have devolved the duties previously performed by the several Chief Magistrates of the different sections of the Territories referred to in the records whose offices have been abolished.

*　　　　　*　　　　　*

In 1894 Pondoland, previously in the position of a British Protectorate, was with the consent of the Chiefs of Eastern and Western Pondoland respectively, annexed to the Cape Colony. Internecine disturbances within the Territory had become a serious menace to the peace and security of the surrounding tribes; the terms of the Maitland Treaty of 1844 had been disregarded and certain barbarous practises connected with witchcraft and "smelling out" were being carried on— such in short were the reasons given for the proposal made to the Pondo Chiefs that they and their people should become British subjects and come under direct British control. A brief period of excitement and uncertainty followed the opening of negotiations. The Chiefs not unnaturally demurred to the proposal that they should part with their independence. The civil officials selected to carry out arrangements were faced with a situation fraught not only with extreme difficulty but also attended with grave personal danger, where the exercise of the utmost tact and patience and a show of the bravest face were the only mediums possible for bringing matters to a successful and peaceful conclusion.

That the terms of cession were eventually signed and the country handed over with no serious show of hostility and without a single shot having been fired is an achievement which does the greatest honour to the handful of officials upon whom the duty of securing the cessions devolved.

After the deeds had been signed, sealed and delivered a detachment of the Cape Mounted Riflemen, some 200 all ranks marched through the country as an outward and visible sign that Pondoland was now British Territory. The country was divided up into Districts in charge of each of which a Magistrate was placed with a small detachment of Cape Mounted Riflemen for Police purposes.

*   *   *

In 1896-1897 the Territories suffered in common with other parts of South Africa from a plague of Rinderpest. Cattle were swept off in thousands. Many people previously prosperous were reduced to abject want. It is gratifying to record that in spite of the disturbing and demoralising effects of losses sustained the people remained calm and met the situation with that stoicism generally attributed to the Native character.

In a remarkably short space of time, districts "burnt out" with Rinderpest began to recover themselves and in a comparatively few years depleted herds so increased as to restore their owners almost to their previous prosperity. A shadow was, however, soon cast over the improved prospects by the approach of East Coast Fever from the North. All that could be done was done to stay its progress but gradually and surely it worked its way South. In 1910 the storm burst. The disease appeared suddenly in one part of the Territories, then as suddenly in others. Measures towards combating its progress were adopted and abandoned, experiments were tried but failed, a period almost of panic ensued and the while the suffering people remained calm. They looked to the white officials for help but none that was effective was forthcoming. Eventually inoculation experiments here and there met with a measure of success.

The scourge in its intensity expended itself but it left in its trail those mouldering fires of infection that we are still trying to quench. At an enormous cost dipping operations on a large scale have been adopted throughout the Territories and though there are sporadic and periodical outbreaks of the disease it is considered on the whole to have been overcome. With a continuation of and persistence in the present methods of eradication there is every reason to hope that ere long the Territories will be enabled to present a clean bill. The Veterinary Officers throughout a most trying and difficult time, working hand in hand with the Magistrates, have brought about a condition of affairs, which, all circumstances and conditions being considered is little short of miraculous.

In 1897 an attempt was made to stir up rebellion among the Griquas. Andrew le Fleur though not a Griqua by birth, had acquired considerable influence in the tribe and was looked up to and supported by a section as principal leader, especially in matters anti-European. In the minds of certain of the older men the happenings connected with the rebellion of '79 were still fresh and, in the person of those who imagined that the people still laboured under injustices and under unredressed grievances, he had material very useful to his objectives, which were the throwing off of the British yoke and the restoration of Griqua independence.

In his enterprise Le Fleur had the secret sympathy of members of surrounding Native tribes, but before his time of action arrived, his plans were discovered and he, with a handful of followers, who endeavoured to escape from Justice, were arrested, taken to King William's Town under escort and there tried and sentenced by the Circuit Court to various terms of imprisonment.

*　　　*　　　*

In 1914 with the outbreak of the Great War a call was made upon the Native people, which met with a prompt and loyal response. Thousands *volunteered* for active service first in West Africa, then in East Africa and in Europe.

Among the dangers to be faced was the crossing of the dreaded ocean. It is difficult for the ordinary European to understand what this would mean to a Native; still, the ready response was "our King is at war, *we wish* to help Him against His enemies." The situation seemed to bring him nearer his Sovereign—his Great Chief—and it was for him to rally round His Person—for such was the popular idea.

Many of those who went on active service, lost their lives from sickness and disease due to great hardships suffered under trying conditions in strange countries. Some were lost at sea—the tragedy of the "Mendi" left many a sorrowing family and destitute home.

Special mention must be made of the Cape Coloured Corps in whose ranks were many representatives from the Transkeian Territories. In the "Near East" the Coloured Corps rendered signal service as an active combatant unit and high mention has been made of the part it played in Mesopotamia. Those Griquas who formed a portion of that unit, were second to none in discipline, in efficiency and in fortitude. They have every reason to be proud of their fighting record.

Meanwhile the European manhood of the Territories, who had responded to the call, left their women and children in perfect safety in their isolated homes, for with the exception of a minor show of disaffection in a particular locality engineered by German propogandists, who had misled a small section of the Natives, life and property were as safe here as were they at that time in any part of the world.

*   *   *

My thanks are due to Miss Shirley Keightley, at one time clerk on the Magisterial staff, Mount Ayliff, for her ever ready assistance in the preparation of these records for the press.

FRANK BROWNLEE.

Mount Ayliff,
July, 1923.

INDEX.

APPENDIX.

TRANSKEI.

(BLUE BOOK, NATIVE AFFAIRS 1885).

The Chief Magistracy of Transkei is a tract of country about two thousand five hundred and thirty-five square miles in extent, lying between the Kei and Bashee Rivers, and extending upwards some seventy miles from the sea. As it does not reach the high terrace of the interior, no portion of it is subject to such cold in winter as to make it unpleasant to natives. Europeans find the heat from November to March somewhat oppressive, but enjoy the climate of the rest of the year. The soil is in general fertile, and the rainfall, which is chiefly derived from thunderstorms in the summer months, is usually sufficient for the production of maize, millet, and garden plants. The country is covered with long grass, and was once adorned with great numbers of mimosa trees, which of late years have been destroyed for fuel. There is still a little valuable timber left in the small forests which are found in recesses of mountains facing seaward.

In 1878 three districts, which for thirteen years previous to that date had been under distinct governments, were united to form this Chief Magistracy. These districts were known as

1. The Idutywa Reserve,
2. Fingoland,
3. Gcalekaland.

Down to the year 1857 these had formed part of the territory occupied by the Gcaleka branch of the Xosa tribe, whose possessions also included the district higher up, now called Emigrant Tembuland. It is therefore necessary to show how we came into contact with the former owners of the land, and to trace the history of our intercourse with them.

By the Europeans who first explored the coast belt of South Africa the Xosa tribe was found to be the advance guard of the Bantu race. In 1686 their outposts extended as far westward as the Keiskama, where they were in contact with clans of Hottentot blood. About the middle of last century the tribe was divided into two great sections by quarrels between Gcaleka and Rarabe, sons of the Chief Palo. Gcaleka was in rank the higher of the two. His adherents occupied the country east of the Kei, while Rarabe secured the allegiance of the clans west of that river, some of which had by that time moved onward as far as the site of the present village of Somerset East. More recently the Rarabes became subdivided into numerous clans, such as the Gaikas, Dlambes, &c., which were frequently at war with each other and with the European settlers who had come to occupy the regions where the Hottentots formerly tended their herds. In 1796 the colonists were obliged to retire to this side of Algoa Bay, and from that year until 1811 the Dlambes held the country to the Sunday River. In 1811 they were driven back, and the Fish River became the boundary. The Rarabe clans, though practically independent, regarded the head of the Gcalekas as their supreme chief, owing to his being the lineal descendant in the great line of the ancient paramount rulers of their tribe

In 1827 the Wesleyan Society founded the mission station of Butterworth in the country of the Gcalekas.   The Revd. Mr. Shrewsbury was the first to occupy the post.   The history of that station would be an account of some of the most stirring events that have happened in South Africa during the last half century, for it would comprise not only the extension of missionary enterprise, but the wanderings and sufferings of the Fingos, and the wars of 1835, 1846-7, and 1851-2, in each of which the mission premises were destroyed.

In 1828 the first intercourse between the Colonial Government and the Gcalekas took place.   In that year the border tribes were threatened with destruction by the advance from the north of the Amangwane or Fetcani, a powerful and ferocious body of invaders. The Cape Government sent an army against these marauders, which put them to flight with great loss.   Hintsa, son of Kawuta and grandson of Gcaleka, with a small body of his followers acted in concert with our forces on this occasion, and the defeat of the Amangwane certainly saved his people as well as the Tembus from being pillaged and dispersed.

In December 1834 the Gaikas and Dlambes, who were still independent of control by our Government, made a sudden attack upon the Colony, and laid waste the frontier districts.   Great herds of cattle fell into their hands, which they drove over the Kei into the Gcaleka country for security.   Following this, some trading stations there were plundered, and one white man was murdered.   Hintsa declined to give any satisfaction, when called upon by Governor Sir Benjamin D'Urban to do so, in consequence of which his country was invaded by our forces.   After some military operations, which were carried out under the direction of Sir Benjamin D'Urban in person and which convinced the Gcalekas that they could not oppose the European troops with any hope of success, Hintsa came to our camp and agreed to terms of peace, which included the surrender of a number of cattle for the due performance of which he volunteered to remain as a hostage.   He had, however, no intention of fulfilling his agreement, and, after leading astray a detachment of our forces under Colonel, (afterwards Sir Harry) Smith, he attempted to make his escape, in which attempt he met his death.   Kreli, his son and heir, was at the time in the colonial camp.   He was at once acknowledged as chief of the Gcalekas, and peace was concluded with him.

This war brought into the race rivalries of the Colony a new competitor, in the Fingos, who now for the first time make their appearance in our history.   When the troops crossed the Kei, they found a large number of people living there in dependence upon the owners of the country, by whom they were treated with contempt and severity. They applied to Sir Benjamin D'Urban for protection, and an arrangement was made that they should be removed to the Colony as British subjects.   These people were the remnants of various tribes which had been broken up a few years earlier by the wars of the Zulu Chief Tshaka.   From the Umzimvubu to the Umvolosi the coast region had been almost depopulated by that renowned warrior, and among others the great tribes of the Amabele, the Amazizi, and the Abambo had been utterly dispersed. Some of the despoiled clans crossed the Drakensberg into the country which is now the Orange Free State, others fled southward along the coast, and sought refuge with the Pondos, Tembus, and Gcalekas. Among themselves these refugees continued to use the old titles of their clans, but by the tribes that gave them shelter they were termed Amafengu (meaning Wanderers) from which word we call them Fingos.

The Fingos differ slightly in appearance and much in disposition from the people of the Xosa tribe. The latter have a taint of Hotten-tot blood in their veins, which gives them a lighter skin, and may be the cause of their greater instability of character. The Fingos were comparatively industrious, as they came from a country where the culture of the soil was depended upon for means of subsistence more than it was by the pastoral clans of the south. The Gcaleka is careless, thriftless, quick tempered, proud, and brave; the Fingo is plodding, calculating, acquisitive, and cold blooded. At first despised on account of their miserable condition, the Fingos soon became detested owing to their talents in overreaching.

In May 1835 some sixteen thousand souls, men, women, and children, migrated under protection of the British troops, and were located by Sir Benjamin D'Urban's instructions in the present Division of Peddie. There they were at first placed under the care of the Revd. John Ayliff, a Wesleyan missionary who had been for some time stationed at Butterworth, and who had been obliged to leave that post and take shelter in Tembuland when the war began. The Fingos brought with them from the Gcaleka country a considerable number of cattle (nearly 30,000) which had been in their charge, a circumstance that tended greatly to increase the hatred with which they were regarded by their former masters.

Kreli never fulfilled the engagements which he contracted when peace was concluded with him by Sir Benjamin D'Urban, and no attempt was made to compel him to do so. This was not entirely his fault. He paid three thousand head of cattle at different times. In December 1835 Sir Benjamin D'Urban reduced the number to which he was entitled by the agreement of the 19th May of that year to twenty-five thousand head of horned cattle and one hundred horses, and called upon the chief to pay these at once. Kreli pleaded inability to collect the cattle, and offered instead to cede to His Majesty's Government in full sovereignty and possession a slip of land from the Kei to the Gona ten miles in width, namely five miles on each side of the great waggon road through Butterworth, together with a circular plot having a radius of seven and a half miles round Butterworth Station, and the right of road without let or hindrance from the Gona to the Bashee with a branch to Clarkebury. Sir Benjamin D'Urban accepted this offer, and in January 1836 the ground was formally handed over by Kreli in presence of his councillors and a large body of attendants, was beaconed off, and was proclaimed British territory by Captain Delaney. But it was restored to Kreli by instructions from Lord

Glenelg, dated 2nd August, 1836, and the chief was thereupon released from all previous engagements.

In 1844 he affixed his mark to a formal treaty of friendship, which was signed by Governor Sir Peregrine Maitland on behalf of Her Britannic Majesty. Under this treaty a subsidy of £50 a year was paid to him. In April 1837 Mr. William Fynn had been stationed with him as Diplomatic Agent, in which capacity he remained for thirteen years, but was unable to exert much influence.

In the war of 1846-7 the Gcalekas took part against the Colony. They could bring no complaint whatever against us, except that we had protected the Fingos; but their sympathy with the Rarabe clans, and the temptation of plunder, led them to take up arms. On this occasion their country was twice entered by our forces, and cattle were taken from them, nearly all of which, however, was really colonial stock which had been swept off by raiders and driven over the Kei for security. At the close of the war, in December 1847, the Rarabe clans were proclaimed British subjects by Governor Sir Harry Smith, and the Province of British Kaffraria was created, with the Kei as its eastern boundary, so that the Gcaleka territory became henceforth contiguous to Her Majesty's dominions.

On the 24th December, 1850, the Gaikas performed the first act in the most formidable rising against British authority which South Africa had yet seen. They were soon joined by numerous Hottentots from the Kat River and deserters from the Cape Mounted Rifles, by a large section of the Tembu tribe, and by various other frontier clans. The Gcalekas also took part against us, though they were unable to produce a single instance of provocation.

It was not until December 1851 that military forces could be spared to cross the Kei, but in that month and in January 1852 the Gcaleka country was scoured, a great number of cattle were recovered, and several thousand Fingos were brought out. Kreli, however, still continued defiant, and refused the terms of peace offered by Sir Harry Smith, which were that he should cease hostilities and pay fifteen hundred head of cattle as compensation for the destruction of the property of missionaries and traders in his country. Soon after this he took part in a raid into the Colony, but was met by Captain Tylden with a burgher force, and was driven back with heavy loss. In August 1852 Governor Sir George Cathcart crossed the Kei with a mixed army of soldiers and burghers, burnt Kreli's kraal, and captured ten thousand head of cattle. This was the virtual close of the war, though it was not until February 1853 that peace was formally concluded with the Gcaleka chief.

From this time for several years to come the only representative of the Imperial or the Colonial Government in the whole country between British Kaffraria and Natal, from the Drakensberg to the sea, was a single officer residing at Morley, who had neither power nor influence. Mr. Matthew B. Shaw, now magistrate of Maclear, was the officer who held the position of British Resident during this period,

In 1856-7 Kreli and his people took the leading part in the destruction of cattle and grain, which was carried out more or less by all the sections of the Xosa tribe, and which must have resulted in a desperate invasion of the Colony if miscalculations on their part and accidents had not prevented it. This insane act ruined the Gcalekas for a time. Great numbers of them perished, and most of those who survived the famine were dispersed in different directions.

Sir George Grey, who was then Governor and High Commissioner, had repeatedly warned Kreli that he would be held responsible for the consequences of inciting the clans under British jurisdiction to destroy their property. In 1858 therefore, to prevent the Gcaleka country being again made a base of attack upon the Colony, Inspector C. D. Griffith was instructed to take possession of it with a body of the Frontier Armed and Mounted Police. Mr. Griffith was joined by a thousand Tembus under the chief Joyi and a party of frontier natives under Colonel Gawler, with whose assistance he drove Kreli and his famished adherents over the Bashee into Bomvanaland.

When this was effected, the natives under Colonel Gawler were located at Idutywa, near the centre of the old Gcaleka country, with the object of assisting to prevent Kreli's return. This was the origin of the present Idutywa district. An officer was stationed there with the title of Transkeian Special Magistrate, who exercised jurisdiction over the people and kept the Government informed of what was going on. Colonel Gawler held this appointment until September 1858, when he was succeeded by Lieutenant George Pomeroy Colley. Mr. W. G. B. Shepstone succeeded Lieutenant Colley in May 1860 and Mr. W. B. Chalmers succeeded Mr. Shepstone in September 1861. Mr. Chalmers held the appointment from that date until the close of 1864. During these seven years the Idutywa district was regarded as a dependency of the Crown Colony of British Kaffraria, and the special magistrates were appointed by the Government of the Province. The natives who settled at Idutywa were offshoots of various clans. About half of them were Fingos, there were some Dlambes under the petty chief Smith Umhala who was a great grandson of Rarabe, and even some Gcalekas. The Idutywa district and the Butterworth mission station were the only portions of the country previously occupied by the Gcalekas which were inhabited during the next seven years. The remainder of the territory was guarded and kept open by the police.

Early in 1862 Sir Philip Wodehouse arrived in South Africa as Governor and High Commissioner. The condition of the frontier was one of the first objects to which he directed his attention, and he was not long in forming a plan for the settlement of the vacant Gcaleka country. The disbanding of the Cape Mounted Rifle Regiment was then contemplated by the Imperial Government, and to increase the strength of the European element in the community, which the reduction of the military establishment seemed to necessitate, the Governor proposed to give out the Transkeian land in farms to occupants under military tenure. Applications for farms were called for, and it was ascertained that there would be no difficulty in filling the country in this manner. The co-operation of the Imperial Government was needed to the extent of providing for a short time a small force of irregular cavalry, at about half the cost of the Cape Mounted Rifles, until the settlers should be in a condition to defend themselves.

While this scheme was being talked about, Kreli was fast regaining importance. His followers were returning to him from the various districts in which they had been scattered by the famine, and Bomvanaland was too small to contain them. The Governor offered him a tract of vacant land in the present district of Maclear, but he declined to accept it. His adherents were beginning to make their way into secluded parts of their old country. In 1864 a panic was created on the frontier, owing to a report that the Gcaleka chief had resolved to attack the police. The rumour reached England, and the Imperial Government, fearing that the occupation of the Transkei by Europeans would necessitate sending troops there, issued instructions in August 1864 that "British dominion must be withdrawn from it, and the Kei be made the extreme boundary."

There were then only two courses left to the Governor: to restore the whole territory to the Gcalekas, or to divide it among different tribes. He chose the latter alternative. Mr. J. C. Warner, an officer in the native department of the colonial service, was instructed to visit Kreli and inform him "that the Government was willing to receive him again into favour and to allow him to re-occupy a portion of the territory, and that he would be paid an allowance of "£100 a year as long as he should conduct himself in a friendly manner." Kreli accepted the offer with many expressions of thanks, and in the months of September and October 1864 his people moved from beyond the Bashee into the country to which the name Gcalekaland has since been restricted. This district was the seaboard portion of that which the Gcalekas occupied before 1857. It extended from the Bashee to the Kei, and from the ocean to the well defined boundary formed partly by flowing water and partly by the great waggon road which runs eastward past Butterworth.

The upper portion of the vacant territory was allotted to a section of the Tembu tribe, and is now included in the Chief Magistracy of Tembuland.

There remained a tract about twelve hundred square miles in extent in the centre of the territory. Sir Philip Wodehouse offered this to the Gaikas under the chiefs Sandili, Anta and Oba, in exchange for their locations west of the Kei, but they declined to accept it. Their principle reason for doing so was an objection to move into a district which the head of their tribe still hoped to acquire, and thus deprive him of it*; but this was not allowed to appear, and Sir Philip Wodehouse was led to believe that they objected to cross the Kei because "they acknowledged the benefits they had received from living in tranquility under our rule, and were indisposed to fall back under the uncontrolled authority of their own chiefs.

*Thirteen years later this was given as their reason by some of the leading men among the Gaikas who declined to move.

The Governor turned next to the Fingos. These people were first introduced to the Colony in 1835, when some sixteen thousand of them were brought across the Kei by Sir Benjamin D'Urban and located in the Peddie district. They had multiplied in an almost incredible manner, there being no parallel in history of any people increasing so rapidly in number as these Fingos have done since they came into the Colony. Their locations in Peddie soon became overcrowded, and swarms from them were then settled in Victoria East, in the beautiful valleys along the Amatolas, and even in the Zitzikama. The same thing went on at each fresh location, so that shortly there was a multitude of Fingos in the border districts, pressing upon the remaining population and clamouring for land.

Sir Philip Wodehouse offered the vacant country to these people, and before the close of the year 1865 nearly forty thousand of them moved into it, without, however, giving up a rood of the land held by Fingos in the Colony. Some of them raised an objection at first to their settlement without protection in a district bordering on that occupied by the Gcalekas, but they were satisfied with a promise that if they conducted themselves properly, Government would not permit their enemies to destroy them. Captain Cobbe, previously Superintendent of Natives at Healdtown, was stationed in Fingoland, as this district has since been termed, with the title of Fingo Agent.

The whole of the territory taken from Kreli in 1858 was thus parcelled out among rival native tribes, and the opportunity of strengthening the European element just where it is most needed to secure peace and progress was thrown away for ever. The Government hoped to be able by its influence alone to preserve order among these people. "In thus disposing of this territory," wrote Sir Philip Wodehouse to the Secretary of State for the Colonies, "we entirely relinquish all rights of Sovereignty over it, and these tribes will be governed by their own chiefs and their own customs. But in accordance with their own wishes, for their benefit as well as for our own, each tribe will be guided and aided by a British Resident."

This quotation shows the nature of the relationship between the Colony and the Transkeian country for several years. There was a British Resident in the person of Mr. J. C. Warner, who was stationed at Idutywa, and who corresponded with the Government and acted generally as a Diplomatic Agent. The only legal authority he possessed was derived from a Commission under the Imperial Act 26 and 27 Victoria c. 35, which empowered him to cause the arrest of criminals being British subjects, anywhere between the Kei and the borders of Natal. Subordinate to him were his son Mr. E. J. Warner, who had the title of Tembu Agent and who resided at Southeyville, Captain Cobbe, who was termed Fingo Agent, and Mr. William Fynn (son of the former Diplomatic Agent with the Gcalekas), who had been for several years clerk to the Special Magistrate at Idutywa, and was appointed Resident with Kreli in July 1865. This arrangement lasted until October 1869, when the office of British Resident was abolished, and the various agents, who had previously reported to Mr. Warner senior, were placed in direct correspondence with the Government.

The natives were not long in discovering that the European officers stationed with them were without any authority, and thereafter only those individuals who could acquire personal influence could be of greater use than mediums of communication. A few extracts from the letters of the Colonial Secretary to the British Resident will give a clear idea of the policy pursued at this time:—

8th November, 1866. "I am directed by the Governor to acknowledge the receipt of your letter of the 15th ultimo, enclosing copies of correspondence with Captain Cobbe, relative to the extent and nature of the authority possessed by him over the Fingos with whom he resides. His Excellency believes it to be essential to the successful working of the Transkeian settlement that the British officers employed there should be perfectly aware that they possess no authority in the legal sense of the word derived from the British Government, inasmuch as Her Majesty's Government have deliberately determined to relinquish the possession they had obtained of that country. The authority of the British officers must therefore strictly speaking be derived altogether from the chiefs and people with whom they dwell, and by whom any directions or advice they may give must be carried into effort. But although it is right that these officers should themselves correctly appreciate their position, it by no means follows that they should bring this circumstance prominently into notice, and thus lower their own influence in dealing with the natives. Each of the tribes settled in the Transkei looks with more or less jealousy on the others. Each desires to retain the good will of the Government. The leading men set a value on the allowances they receive. The individuals composing each tribe have become alive to the benefits of an impartial administration, and have probably little desire to come under the uncontrolled power of their chiefs. All these influences will operate to sustain the authority of the British Resident, and to enable him to procure the execution of orders given with discretion and with a due regard for the habits and prejudices of the native races."

4th March, 1867. "His Excellency has directed me to say that notwithstanding whatever may have been, or may now be, His Excellency's opinion as to the legality or expediency of appointing Special Magistrates beyond the Kei, the retention of officers in that country styled Magistrates would not be viewed with satisfaction by Her Majesty's Government, and consequently His Excellency has no other course to adopt than to obey the instructions conveyed to him. I am to add that if the people of the Reserve (Idutywa) are desirous that you should continue to exercise control over them there is nothing to prevent your continuing to do so as heretofore, on the understanding that in the issue of any judicial orders it will rest with the people whether they are willing to comply with them, it being distinctly understood that the orders cannot be enforced by any authority derived from the Government of this Colony."

10th August, 1868. "The Government does not profess to exercise the authority of law over these people (the Fingos), or to claim the right of enforcing its decisions, further than as they may be acceptable to the people themselves, and be adopted and carried out by them."

7th October, 1868. "The Transkeian arrangement was made because Her Majesty's Government declined to take possession of the country as British territory, and the tribes or portions of tribes now settled there went over with a knowledge that such was the case, and because they would be free from British law and positive authority."

The system indicated in the above extracts gave very little satisfaction either to the colonists or the more advanced natives. The Fingos, who during their residence in the Colony had made great strides in civilization, were now rapidly falling back into the habits of their ancestors. In the wars of Tshaka they had lost most of their chiefs, so that it was much less difficult for them than for other natives to adopt European ideas. They were of various clans, and had no bond of union except to the Government of the white man, while they were surrounded by enemies ever ready to pounce upon and destroy them. Their best men admitted their inability to form a Government of their own, and were desirous of some better system than one in which the only means of coercion was the stoppage of a paltry allowance to the head of a kraal or letting loose the people of one village to plunder those of another. Captain Cobbe was withdrawn in May 1869, and after a short interval during which Mr. C. J. Levey was in charge of the office, Captain Blyth was appointed Fingo Agent. This officer, who was possessed of great ability as a native administrator, not only arrested the downward movement of the Fingos by the influence which he rapidly acquired over them, but smoothed the way for the next important change and drew the people willingly with him.

When the office of British Resident was abolished, Mr. Thomas A. Cumming was stationed at Idutywa with the title of Superintendent. The people of that district were refugees of various tribes, without any chief of rank among them. Those who did not submit to be ruled by the Superintendent were in a state of anarchy.

While matters were in this condition a change took place in the Government of the Cape Colony, by which the direction of native affairs was confided to officers responsible to the Colonial Parliament. This carried with it a change in the method of dealing with the Transkeian tribes; and an attempt to bring them under control and oblige them to contribute towards the expense of their government was very shortly made. There was no difficulty in inducing the inhabitants of Fingoland and Idutywa to consent to pay taxes. Under Captain Blyth's influence the Fingos had already laid a tax upon themselves of £1,500 towards the establishment of an Industrial Institution in connection with the mission of the Free Church of Scotland, which amount they subsequently increased to £4,500. In 1874 they and the people of Idutywa of their own free will began to pay a hut tax of ten shillings a year.

The Government then brought before the Cape Parliament the question of the annexation to the Colony of the districts of Fingoland and Idutywa, and in the session of 1875 a resolution declaring the advisability of this measure was adopted by both Houses. In the following year Letters Patent were issued by Her Majesty, authorising the Governor to proclaim those districts annexed to the Colony after an Act for that purpose should be passed. In the session of 1877 the Cape Parliament passed the Act required, but it was not until the first of October, 1879, that it was brought into effect by the Governor's proclamation.

The district which was restored to Kreli in 1864, and thenceforth called Gcalekaland, was not annexed to the Colony. By their own desire the Gcalekas remained independent, and the colonial officer stationed with them merely performed duties similar to those of a consul, without interfering with their government. Their wars with the Tembus at this time will be referred to in the account of the Chief Magistracy of Tembuland. In May 1873 Mr. William Fynn was succeeded as Resident with Kreli by Mr. James Ayliff. Mr. Ayliff was transferred to Fingoland in March 1876, and in November of that year Colonel Eustace assumed the duty, the clerk, Mr. West Fynn, having acted as Resident during the interval.

At the time when Colonel Eustace became Resident with Kreli there was a general feeling of uneasiness throughout the frontier districts of the Colony. The natives had been arming, and their tone and bearing indicated that a collision was probable at no distant date. Kreli at that time had some twelve thousand warriors at his command, without counting those of the kindred clans west of the Kei. Maki, his former chief councillor, a moderate and sensible man whose weight was always on the side of peace, had been accused of being a sorcerer, and had been compelled to flee to Idutywa for safety. His place was then filled by Ngubo, commander of the Gcaleka army and a near relative of the chief, whose strongest feeling was one of bitter hostility to the white man. The tribe had increased until the territory, which in 1864 was ample for its requirements, was now too small; and jealous eyes were cast over the Fingo border. One circumstance which weakened the Gcalekas, however, was the very bad feeling which then existed between Kreli and his cousin Mapasa, a chief of high rank, and considerable power. Mapasa was the great son of Bukhu, who was son and heir of the right hand house of Kawuta. In such a condition of affairs, the least rumour, however unfounded, is capable of causing alarm among a people so unprotected as the frontier colonists then were. The panic of 1876 passed away, indeed, but a general sense of insecurity remained.

On the 3rd of August 1877 there was a marriage party at a Fingo kraal just within the border, and two petty Gcaleka chiefs, by name Umxoli and Fihla, with a small party of attendants crossed over to partake in the festivities. On such occasions custom demands that all who attend are to be made welcome. In the evening, when all were excited with dancing and beer drinking, a quarrel arose, no one was afterwards able to tell exactly how or why. At any rate the Gcalekas were ranged on one side and the Fingos on the other, and they used their sticks so freely that one Gcaleka was killed and two chiefs were badly bruised. The visitors were then driven over the border.

Three days later four large parties of Gcalekas, who had in the meantime mustered with the intention of avenging the insult offered to their friends, crossed into Fingoland, and swept off the stock belonging to several villages along the line. Mr. Ayliff, the Fingo Agent, and Colonel Eustace, the Resident with Kreli, endeavoured to prevent the disturbance spreading, but the excitement on both sides was now so great that all were deaf to reason. The raids of the Gcalekas being continued, detachments of the Frontier Armed and Mounted Police were sent to protect the Fingos. Colonel Griffith, then Governor's Agent in Basutoland, was hastily summoned to take command of the colonial forces. Volunteers were called to the front. The first battalion of the 24th Regiment, commanded by Colonel Glyn, was disposed at different defensive posts on the western side of the Kei, to prevent a raid into the colony. Governor Sir Bartle Frere proceeded to Butterworth, and endeavoured, but without success, to induce Kreli to meet him and come to some amicable arrangement.

On the 23rd of September, on account of Kreli's plain declaration that he could not restrain his people, all attempts at negotiation were abandoned, and Colonel Eustace withdrew to the police station at Ibeka. Up to this time the Gcalekas had constantly asserted that they were making war upon the Fingos only, but on the 26th an army five thousand strong crossed the border and attacked the police under Inspector Chalmers at Guadana. Mr. Chalmers had eighty Europeans and fifteen hundred Fingos with him. The carriage of his only field piece broke down, when the Fingos dispersed, and he was obliged to retire to Ibeka. A sub-inspector and six men fell in this action. On the 29th and again on the 30th the police camp at Ibeka, where Colonel Griffith was then in command, was attacked by a Gcaleka army variously estimated from six to ten thousand strong. After severe fighting, the assailants were beaten off with heavy loss.

By this time volunteers were arriving from different parts of the Colony, and in the first week in October Colonel Griffith found himself in command of 580 Police, and 620 Volunteer Cavalry, and 370 Volunteer Infantry. On the 3rd of October Major Elliot arrived with a contingent of Gangelizwe's Tembus. A large Fingo force under Mr. Ayliff was also in the field.

The chief Mapasa had in the meantime abandoned the Gcaleka cause and sought protection from the Government. A portion of his clan followed him, but many of his best warriors, led by his nephew Kiva, joined Kreli's army. Those who adhered to Mapasa went across the Kei, where it was found that they numbered 4,315 individuals of all ages.

On the 9th October the Gcalekas were defeated by Colonel Griffith in an engagement at Kreli's kraal, and on the same day the Kaffrarian

Volunteers under Commandant Grey were successful in an engagement at the Springs. On the 22nd the battle of Lusizi was fought, and by the end of the month the Gcalekas were driven over the Bashee. In the engagements mentioned here and in several skirmishes they had lost some seven hundred men killed. Thirteen thousand head of horned cattle, together with a good many horses, sheep and goats, had been captured by our forces. The Gcaleka army was pursued into Pondoland, and then, as it was believed that Kreli's power was completely broken, the colonial forces returned to Ibeka, where most of the Volunteers were disbanded and the police went into quarters.

While the military operations were being performed, a proclamation was issued by Governor, Sir Bartle Frere, (5th October, 1877) in which Kreli was deposed from all power and authority as a chief. His country was taken from him and reserved for disposal as the Government should direct, and pending instructions from her Majesty's Government it was to be ruled by Officers appointed by the Government of the Cape of Good Hope. This proclamation was approved of by the Secretary of State for the Colonies in a despatch of the 14th November following, and is the basis upon which the administration of Gcalekaland rests.

It was soon made evident that the Volunteers had been too hastily disbanded. The Gcalekas, though they had suffered severe losses, were by no means disheartened, and having placed their women, children, and cattle in safety, they returned to renew the war. On the 2nd of December their presence was made known by an attack upon a detachment of Police and Volunteers, 152 strong, which was marching towards the Kei and had halted at a place called Holland's Shop. Inspector Bourne, who was in command, formed his men into a hollow square flanked with guns, and succeeded in beating off his assailants.

In the campaign of October the Imperial troops had garrisoned the posts west of the Kei while the colonial forces were engaged in Gcalekaland, but now a different arrangement was made. Colonel Glyn, of the 24th, was placed in command over the Kei ; and his own regiment, part of the 88th which was hurried up from Cape Town, and a naval brigade from Her Majesty's ship *Active,* took the field under his orders. Auxiliary corps of Fingos and Tembus were raised, and the work of clearing the country of the Gcalekas was again commenced.

This was hardly begun when the area of disturbance was enormously enlarged by the rising of many of the Rarabe clans. On the 22nd of December the Gcaleka chief Kiva crossed the Kei and entered the Gaika Location. Sandile's people took up arms at once, and they were imitated by various clans until the battle ground extended as far westward as Fort Beaufort and as far northward as Queenstown.

Owing to the rebellion of the Rarabes, the campaign in Gcalekaland could not be carried on with as much vigour as at first, but during December 1877 and January 1878 a good deal of skirmishing took place, in which the enemy was invariably worsted. On the 7th of February 1878 the decisive battle of Kentani took place. Captain Upcher, who was in charge of the Kentani post, had 436 Europeans of the Imperial and Colonial services and about 560 Fingos under his command. He was attacked by about five thousand Gcalekas and Gaikas, and an engagement took place in which the casualties on his side were only two Fingos killed and two Europeans and seven Fingos wounded, but which cost the enemy some 300 of his bravest men. They came on in dense masses, and were mown down by a fire from heavy guns. Both Kreli and Sandile were present in this engagement. The principal column was led by Xito, the shaman or tribal priest* of the Gcalekas, who had performed certain ceremonies which caused the warriors to believe that they were invulnerable; but this feeling of confidence being destroyed, they gave way to despair. When they broke and fled, the Volunteer cavalry and the Fingos pursued and prevented them rallying. The battle of Kentani was a decisive one. Kreli did not attempt any further resistance, but with his remaining adherents at once crossed the Bashee.

The whole of the present Chief Magistracy thus came under the control of the Colonial Government, but the recently acquired portion was held under a different tenure from that of Fingoland and Idutywa. These last named districts were annexed to the Colony, for though the Governor's proclamation was not yet issued, it was only delayed by a pressure of business of greater importance. Gcalekaland was territory obtained by conquest, but not annexed to the Colony. The civil officers in the territory at this time were Mr. James Ayliff, whose title had been altered from Fingo Agent to Chief Magistrate of Fingoland, Mr. T. P. Pattle, who had been appointed Assistant Magistrate and stationed at Butterworth in September 1877, Mr. F. P. Gladwin, who had been appointed Assistant Magistrate and stationed at Tsomo in October 1877, and Mr. T. R. Merriman, who in February 1878 had succeeded Mr. T. A. Cumming at Idutywa, with the title of magistrate.

In September 1878 the arrangements were completed under which the government of the country has ever since been carried on. The three territories of Idutywa, Fingoland, and Gcalekaland were united, and Captain Blyth, C.M.G., who had been successively Fingo Agent and Chief Magistrate of Griqualand East, was appointed Chief Magistrate of the Transkei.

---

* " Witchdoctor " is the term commonly used by colonists to signify the holder of this office, but the word is not a good one. Xito's duties were to perform sacrifices for the tribe on important occasions, to prepare the warriors for battle, and to "smell out" those who sought to inflict injury on the Chief's house by means of witchraft. Under the fifteenth clause of the Regulations for the government of Transkei, Tembuland, and Griqualand East, such individuals as Xito are liable to punishment for the performance of the last mentioned of these duties. The clause reads: Any person falsely accusing another of practising witchcraft, or other such acts, shall be guilty of an offence punishable as in the last preceding regulations provided (fine, or imprisonment with or without spare diet and with or without solitary confinement, or whipping not exceeding thirty-six lashes, or by all or any such punishment).

Fingoland was divided into three sub-magistracies, namely Nqama-kwe, Tsomo, and Butterworth. In October Mr. Gladwin was removed from Tsomo and appointed magistrate of Nqamakwe. In December Mr. Pattle was removed from Butterworth to Tsomo, and at the same time Mr. T. A. King was appointed magistrate of Butterworth.

Idutywa remained as before a single district, of which Mr. T. R. Merriman continued to be the magistrate.

Gcalekaland was divided into two districts, named Kentani and Willowvale. Those Gaikas who had taken no part in the rebellion were removed from the old location west of the Kei, and ground was assigned to them in the district of Kentani. It was intended to intro-duce the system of individual tenure, and to assign ten acres of arable land, to each head of a family, with grazing rights over extensive commonages; but this plan has not yet been carried out. Four blocks of land, each twenty thousand acres in extent, were selected as loca-tions, and upon them the immigrant Gaikas were placed, numbering 1,019 men, 2,278 women, and 4,367 children. Mr. M. B. Shaw was appointed magistrate of this district, and assumed duty on the 1st of October. The only legal power which he could exercise was derived from a commission under the Act 26 and 27 Victoria c. 35, but practi-cally he had the same jurisdiction as the sub-magistrates of Fingoland and Idutywa.

In the district of Willowvale a considerable number of Gcalekas, who surrendered their arms and professed their willingness to come under colonial jurisdiction, were located. Mr. F. N. Streatfeild, C.M.G., was appointed magistrate of this district, and assumed duty on the 2nd of January 1879. His powers *de jure* and *de facto* were the same as those of Mr. Shaw.

Some considerable areas of land in these districts, Kentani and Willowvale, were reserved for occupation by Europeans, but only a few individuals have as yet been located there.

In 1879 the residents of Idutywa and Fingoland were required to surrender their arms to the Government, for which they received com-pensation in money. In October 1880 many of the clans beyond the Bashee rose in rebellion. At that time the only military force in the Transkei consisted of three Cape Mounted Riflemen stationed at Ibeka. The rebels were in expectation of being joined by the Fingos, who were known to be brooding over their disarmament, which they felt as a grievance. The Fingos, however, saw at once that a coalition with the rebels, if successful, would be followed by their own destruction, and the Christian section set an example to the rest by responding to Captain Blyth's call for volunteers to enrol under European officers for the defence of the border.

On the 10th of November (1880) a body of rebels made a raid into Fingoland and killed Captain Blakeway and about thirty of the Fingos under his command. On the 14th of November a second raid was made, when Captain Von Linsingen, his son, and three other Europeans were killed. Shortly after this the colonial forces arrived at the scene of disturbance, and prevented a repetition of these attacks. A large force of Fingos was subsequently employed in assisting to suppress the rebellion, and in that duty performed good service.

Though the districts of Nqamakwe, Tsomo, Butterworth, and Idutywa are annexed to the Colony, colonial law is not carried out in them as it is on this side of the Kei. Under the conditions of annexation the Governor-in-Council was empowered to draw up regulations which should have the force of law. These regulations were to be published in the Gazette, and in the session following their publication be laid before Parliament, which retained the power of repealing, altering, or varying them. No Acts of the Cape Parliament were to be in force unless proclaimed so by the Governor, or expressly extended to the annexed districts in the Acts themselves. The code published in 1879 is the whole body of colonial law then in existence, except when in conflict with a number of regulations issued at the same time. One of these regulations is that where all parties to a civil suit are natives the case may be dealt with according to native law, that is recognised custom.

The jurisdiction of the magistrates is unlimited in civil cases, but the loser has the right of appeal to the Chief Magistrate, or (since 1882) to the Eastern Districts Court, or the Supreme Court, as he may choose. In criminal cases the magistrates have large powers, but their decisions are subject to review by the Chief Magistrate, and since 1882 appeals can be made to the judges of the Supreme Court exactly as in the older districts of the Colony. Persons charged with the commission of crimes to which by the colonial law the penalty of death is attached were formerly tried by a court consisting of the Chief Magistrate as President and two of the sub-magistrates. Since the Act No. 40 of 1882 became law, such persons are sent for trial to the nearest town where a session of the Circuit Court is held.

Since February 1882 the Fingos have voluntarily paid an annual tax of Two Shillings and Six Pence each man for local purposes. This "Fingoland District Fund" is administered by a committee of headmen and magistrates, who meet once every three months at the office of the Chief Magistrate. There are also sub-committees which meet monthly at each magistracy. The proceeds of this tax amount to about £800 annually, and the Government contributes from the general revenue a sum equal to that voluntarily raised. The fund is devoted to the maintenance of a hospital,* the construction and repair of roads, and such other public works as the committee may determine. This is a striking proof of the advancement in civilization which is being made by the Fingos under Captain Blyth's guidance.

From the time that Gcalekaland came into our possession, its annexation to the Colony has been considered advisable, in order that the system of Government might be made legally uniform throughout the Chief Magistracy. In the session of the Cape Parliament in 1878 a

---

* This hospital is at Butterworth, and receives patients from all parts of the Chief Magistracy. In 1884 the inhabitants of each of the districts of Idutywa, Kentani, and Willowvale agreed to contribute £50 yearly towards its support.

resolution proposed by the Secretary for Native Affairs in the House of Assembly was agreed to: " that in the opinion of this House it is "expedient that . . . . . Gcalekaland . . . . . should be annexed to "this Colony, and that the Government take such steps as may place it "in a position to introduce a Bill to effect such annexation."

On the 9th of January 1879 Sir Bartle Frere, in a despatch to the Secretary of State, forwarded this resolution, and on behalf of the colonial Ministry requested that Her Majesty's Government would sanction the annexation. At that time the Imperial Government was anxious to bring about a confederation of the South African Colonies and States, similar to that of the Canadian Dominion. Sir Michael Hicks Beach therefore replied that he was disposed to think the present hardly a convenient time for taking any steps for determining the future position of Gcalekaland, and that it would seem preferable to wait until the general principles of confederation could be settled by a conference of colonial delegates. On the 19th of May Sir Bartle Frere wrote again, strongly recommending that the request of the Cape Parliament should be complied with, so as to enable legislation to proceed in the coming session. The Secretary of State answered that he could not comply, as Her Majesty's Government was very anxious that all questions connected with the territories adjacent to the Cape Colony, and not as yet actually incorporated with it, should be considered in connection with the delimitation of the Provinces of the proposed Union.

The session of 1879 thus passed by without the possibility of an Annexation Act being introduced. The correspondence with the Secretary of State was, however, continued, in despatches too numerous for each to be referred to. On the 21st of October the Governor forwarded a Minute of the Ministry, in which they stated that they deemed it of the utmost importance that the country formerly occupied by Kreli and the Gcalekas should be annexed to the Colony. At last, on the 29th of January 1880 Sir Michael Hicks Beach wrote to Sir Bartle Frere that he had advised Her Majesty to issue Letters Patent under the Great Seal authorising the Colonial Parliament to proceed with the necessary legislation, and that the Letters Patent would be transmitted as soon as certain assurances were received from the Colonial Ministry. On the 24th of March he wrote that he was satisfied with the assurances which had been forwarded, but desired that the code of regulations for the government of the territory should be submitted to him before the annexation was completed. On the 3rd of May Earl Kimberley, who had in the meantime succeeded Sir Michael Hicks Beach, forwarded a telegram to Sir Bartle Frere, announcing that the Letters Patent authorising the annexation would be transmitted as soon as they had been settled by the law officers.

In the session of 1880 an Annexation Act was passed by the Cape Parliament, but now another difficulty arose. The Secretary of State declined to advise Her Majesty to assent to it, owing to some confusion about the code of regulations and the report of a Commission then about to be appointed to enquire into native laws and customs. A change of Ministry at the Cape followed, and further delays occurred until the Bill fell through by effluxion of time.

In the session of 1884 the question was taken up *de novo*, and a resolution similar to that of 1878 was adopted by the Parliament.

In the meantime the districts of Kentani and Willowvale are practically in a position differing but little from the remainder of the Chief Magistracy. The Governor of the Cape Colony holds a separate Commission as Governor of Gcalekaland and other native territories similarly situated, and is guided by the advice of the Colonial Ministry. The administration of these districts is carried on through the Native Department, and the revenue and expenditure are regulated by the Parliament just as if they were legally districts of the Colony. The Act No. 40 of 1882 does not, however, apply to them.

The population of the Chief Magistracy of Transkei cannot be given with any pretension to accuracy. In 1879, according to a census carefully taken, it consisted of 83,182 souls. Since that date there has been not alone the natural increase to account for, but a considerable immigration from the districts this side of the Kei. The Chief Magistrate believes that the people under his charge now exceed one hundred thousand in number.

The Colonial Government has at present (exclusive of military and police) the following European Officers in the Transkei: a Chief Magistrate, six sub-magistrates, one accountant, six clerks, and a District Surgeon.

Captain Blyth, C.M.G., holds the appointment of Chief Magistrate, (From the 1st of March 1883 to the 13th of September 1884 Captain Blyth was absent, and Mr. D. Hook was Acting Chief Magistrate).

The following list shows the succession of sub-Magistrates:—

NQAMAKWE: Mr. F. P. Gladwin.
  Mr. T. A. King, April 1881.
TSOMO: Mr. T. P. Pattle.
  Mr. T. A. King, June 1880.
  A clerk acting, April 1881.
  Mr. W. Girdwood, July 1881.
  Mr. M. W. Liefeldt, July 1883.
  Mr. N. O. Thompson, October 1884.
BUTTERWORTH: Mr. T. A. King.
  Mr. T. R. Merriman, June 1880.
  Mr. R. W. Stanford, May 1884.
IDUTYWA: Mr. T. R. Merriman.
  Mr. T. P. Pattle, June 1880.
  Mr. C. G. H. Bell, January 1882
KENTANI: Mr. M. B. Shaw.
  Mr. W. Girdwood, July 1883.
  Mr. A. W. Fuller, November 1884.
WILLOWVALE: Mr. F. N. Streatfeild, C.M.G.
  Mr. M. W. Liefeldt, October 1884.

The total revenue accounted for in the Chief Magistracy of Transkei from the 1st of July 1879 to the 31st of December 1883 was £47,670 8s. 7d. The expenditure during these four years and a half (excluding military, against which customs duty not collected in the Territory may be placed) was £160,548 11s 10d. The balance of expenditure over revenue during that period was therefore £112,878 3s. 3d., and retrenchment was thus a matter of the most urgent necessity. In one item alone,—grants in aid of mission schools, no less a sum than £18,249 8s. 3d. had been expended, that is to say thirty-eight per cent. of the entire revenue had been devoted to educational purposes. In public works during the same period £41,478 16s. 4d had been expended, or a sum equal to eighty-seven hundredths of the revenue.

The revenue for the year from 1st January to 31st December 1884 was £15,891 0s. 4d., made up of the following items: Land (Hut Tax, etc.) £11,610 10s. 6d., Fines, Forfeitures, &c., £1,768 18s. 3d., Licences £1,169 2s. 6d., Stamps £856 17s. 11d., Telegraph Receipts £190 11s. 7d. and Miscellaneous Receipts £294 19s. 7d.

The expenditure for civil purposes in the Chief Magistracy during the year ending 31st December 1884 cannot be given with absolute accuracy, as the ordinary expenditure accounts for the month of November and December are not yet audited as this goes to press. It is thus possible that the total may be affected by a few shillings or even pounds. The figures given provisionally by the Audit Office are:—

Ordinary Expenditure	...	...	£15,147	12	6
Education	...	...	...	4,743	11	5
Stationery	...	...	...	87	18	3
Survey Expenses	...	...	...	820	3	8
Telegraphs	...	...	...	635	19	7
Post Offices	...	...	...	433	1	1
			£21,868	6	6

In addition to the above, the sum of £7,820 0s. 8d. was expended for public works in the three Chief Magistracies of Transkei, Tembuland, and Griqualand East during 1884, but the accounts have not yet been adjusted so as to determine what proportion is chargeable to each.

These figures show that a great advance has been made towards the equalization of revenue and expenditure, but the reductions have so recently come into operation that their effect is not yet fully apparent. The educational grants are still, it will be observed, nearly thirty per cent of the revenue. As will be seen in the Chief Magistrate's report, it is estimated that in the current year the receipts and disbursements will be about equal.

The following genealogical table of the Chiefs of the Ama-Xosa will show the relationship between the Gcalekas, Gaikas, and Dlambes:—

XOSA (From him the tribe has its name).

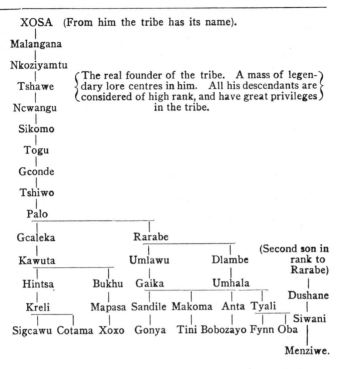

Malangana

Nkoziyamtu

Tshawe { The real founder of the tribe. A mass of legen-
dary lore centres in him. All his descendants are
considered of high rank, and have great privileges }
in the tribe.

Ncwangu

Sikomo

Togu

Gconde

Tshiwo

Palo

Gcaleka   Rarabe

Kawuta   Umlawu   Dlambe   (Second son in
                                                 rank to
Hintsa   Bukhu   Gaika   Umhala   Rarabe)

Kreli   Mapasa Sandile Makoma Anta Tyali   Dushane

Sigcawu Cotama Xoxo Gonya Tini Bobozayo Fynn Oba Siwani

                                                 Menziwe.

(GEO. M. THEAL.)

TEMBULAND.

(BLUE BOOK ON NATIVE AFFAIRS 1885).

The Chief Magistracy of Tembuland covers an area of about four thousand and fifty-five square miles. It is an irregularly shaped block of ground, half encircling the Transkeian Chief Magistracy, and extending from the Drakensberg to the sea. It occupies the space between the Transkeian Chief Magistracy, the Divisions of Queenstown, Wodehouse and Barkly, Griqualand East and Pondoland.

The high lands along the base of the Drakensberg enjoy a healthy and pleasant climate. They are subject to occasional droughts, but usually the rainfall, which is chiefly derived from thunderstorms in summer, is ample for the requirements of agriculture. Hoar frost is common in winter, and snow frequently falls on the mountains. In mid-summer the heat is unpleasant at times, but is rarely oppressive. These uplands afford excellent pasturage for sheep and horned cattle, and a large portion of the ground along the margins of streams is adapted for agriculture.

The low lands along the coast between the Bashee and the Umtata are much less pleasant for Europeans. The heat in summer is very oppressive, and there are certain localities which, owing to the bad quality of the water, have the reputation of being unhealthy. The natives, however, do not seem to be affected by the climate. Horned cattle thrive in this district, but horses and sheep perish quickly when brought into it.

The Chief Magistracy of Tembuland, as at present constituted, consists, like that of the Transkei, of three sections, each of which needs separate notice. They are called

1. Emigrant Tembuland,
2. Tembuland Proper,
3. Bomvanaland.

The first two of these sections are inhabited principally by people acknowledging the same paramount chief, but they came under our government at different times and in different ways. The last is occupied by a distinct tribe.

The Abatembu as they term themselves, the Tembus or Tambookies as we term them, were found by shipwrecked seamen in 1688 occupying the country between the Bashee and the Umtata rivers, and there they were still living at the commencement of the present century. The tribe was composed of many clans, each governed by a chief with large powers over his immediate followers, but all more or less subject to the paramount authority of the head of the family descended from Tembu. Some of these clans were very small, others were powerful; some depended directly upon the paramount chief, others were grouped under a sub-chief who was their superior but was himself a vassal of the head of the tribe.

This form of government, which is common to all the Bantu tribes, is inherently weak; and in the case of the Tembus it was particularly frail, owing to the fact that many of the clans were of alien blood. Where all the sections of the tribe, as is the case with the Xosas, are under chiefs descended from one common ancestor, the bond of religion tends to keep them together. There is an individual recognised by each clan as the tribal priest, who offers sacrifices on all important occasions to the spirits of their dead chiefs, and who exercises enormous influence over every member of the tribe.

But this powerful element of union is wanting where a tribe is composed of clans of different origin, unless time and favourable circumstances have welded them together. The religion of the people is of the same nature, but the object of propitiation is different. The influence of the individual who offers the sacrifices does not extend beyond the clans whose chiefs are descendants of one family. There are in fact as many such individuals as there are ruling families whose relationship cannot be traced. The alien clan consults only temporal interests, and is not prevented by religious scruples from rebelling against its paramount chief. A tribe so constituted may be kept together by the nominal head preserving a balance of power among the sections, but it has little military strength. In this respect the Tembus were not inherently so weak as, for instance, the Pondos; but they were far from being as strong as the compact Xosas.

The wars of Tshaka extended as far as to the Tembu tribe. That great Zulu conqueror sent an army into their country, which traversed it without meeting any opposition, as the Tembus fled on the approach of such renowned assailants. Much greater loss was inflicted by the Amangwane, a tribe that migrated from Zululand and, after devastating the Basuto country, crossed the Drankensberg and fell upon the Tembus. To prevent the Colony from being overrun by hordes of famishing savages, assistance was then sent to the people who were threatened with destruction, and in August 1828 the Amangwane were routed and nearly exterminated by a combined military and burgher commando aided by bodies of Tembu and Gcaleka warriors.

The disturbances of this period caused many of the clans to remove from their original homes. They migrated into a country previously occupied only by a few wandering Bushmen, but which is now the Colonial Division of Queenstown. The chief of highest rank among the emigrant clans was named Bawana. He was a distant relative of Vusani, then the paramount chief of the Tembu tribe.

Among these people the Moravian Society established the mission station of Shiloh, where in January 1837 a treaty of peace and friendship was concluded between Sir Andries Stockenstrom, for the King of England, and Mapasa, son of Bawana, for his people. Mr. Henry Fynn was then for a short time stationed with the emigrant clans as diplomatic agent. The treaty of 1837 was amended in 1841 by another concluded at Grahamstown between Sir George Napier and Mapasa. This again was annulled in 1845 by a treaty, to which Mapasa was a party, between Sir Peregrine Maitland and Umtirara, who had succeeded his father Vusani as paramount chief of the Tembu In this treaty the Governor engaged to pay the contracting chiefs £100 yearly either in money or useful articles as long as they should observe it and remain the faithful allies of Her Majesty.

This treaty did not prevent Mapasa from aiding the Rarabe clans against the Colony in the war of 1846-7. He seems to have been led into the fray principally by the temptation of plunder, though, as his people had lived for so many years near to the Gaikas and a good many intermarriages had taken place, there was much sympathy between them. In a raid into the Colony he managed to drive off a large number of cattle, but most of these were in turn taken from him by Umtirara, who was desirous of securing the assistance of the Colonial Government against his enemies. He therefore made a selection of three hundred of the best cattle among those taken by Mapasa, and proceeded with them to the camp of Sir Peregrine Maitland, where the village of Alice has since been built. There he requested to be taken under the protection of the Queen of England, and offered the three hundred oxen as a proof of his fidelity. The cattle were accepted as restored colonial stock. Sir P. Maitland took into consideration the question of receiving the Tembus under British protection, but Sir Henry Pottinger, who soon after this succeeded him, rejected the proposal.

In April 1847 Mr. E. M. Cole was appointed Commissioner with the Tembus, but the office was abolished in February 1849.

Before the war of 1851-2 Umtirara died, leaving his heir Qeya, or Gangelizwe as he is now termed, a minor. The portion of the tribe living between the Bashee and the Umtata then came under the government of Joyi, a brother of the deceased chief, acting as regent. Nonesi, widow of Vusani, took up her residence among the emigrant clans, and acted as chief over some of them.* When the war commenced, Mapasa and the clans subjected to him joined the Xosas against the Colony, and Nonesi and her adherents withdrew to the section of the tribe of which Joyi was regent. There had long been a feeling of jealousy between the Tembu and Xosa tribes, and at this very time Nonesi and Joyi were professing the strongest friendship towards the Colony. Was Mapasa then acting contrary to their wishes and to what they believed to be the interests and duties of their people?

In a Kafir tribe one clan is frequently found fighting against another, and the paramount chief looks on at first with as much composure as if they were engaged in a lawsuit. By and by, however, he and his councillors consider that one of the parties has been punished sufficiently, or that the quarrel has gone far enough, and an order to observe the peace is issued. The refusal to respect such an order is considered rebellion, but the instances are very rare in which the great chief's messenger is not immediately obeyed, unless the clan is of alien blood and is only a portion of the tribe by adoption.

---

*Nonesi was a daughter of the Pondo Chief Faku and great wife of Vusani or Ngubencuka as he was sometimes called. She had no children, so Umtirara was transferred from a minor to the great house, and succeeded his father as paramount chief.

War may be carried on between two clans of different tribes without involving their paramount chiefs, as long as these choose to look upon it as a mere local fray. As soon, however, as one of the paramount chiefs comes to consider his vassal as wronged or the interests of his tribe as affected, he calls upon the other paramount chief to make peace. He does not deal directly with the other's vassal, but holds the chief of the tribe responsible for the deeds of all its members To follow native custom. our Government should have called upon Joyi and Nonesi to keep Mapasa in order, and if they did not do it, should have attacked them.

But long before this date the natives had discovered that our custom differed greatly from theirs and that war with us was similar to a common game of their boys. In this game some of the youths represent wild animals, and others are hunters. A plot of ground is marked off and called "the bush." Anyone representing an animal can get breathing time if he can manage to get into the bush, where he is safe from molestation. When the son of a chief is present, a small area round his person is the bush.

The natives had discovered that we recognise the existence of the bush in war, and henceforth they took care to provide one, though they took equally good care that we should know nothing about it. The great chief is the bush. He declares that he is a man of peace and is sitting still, that his people will not obey his orders, and if his heart could be seen it would be found full of friendship, that he regards the Queen as his mother, &c., &c. In the meantime his people fight. If as hunters they win, they bring him the spoil. If as hunted they want breathing time, they go to him for shelter.

This was the position of the Tembu Regency in 1851-2. To them the issue of the struggle was doubtful, for they had no conception of the resources of the Empire, and never before in South Africa had there been so many foes arrayed against it. They were jealous of the Amaxosa, but what if these should win! And so Mapasa became Kreli's ally and helped to plunder the Colony, though his army was not so large as it would have been if the sympathy of the tribe had been wholly with him ; and Nonesi and Joyi became the bush to which, if necessary, the warriors could retire for shelter. This position admitted also that if it became apparent that Kreli would be beaten, they could secure some of the spoil for themselves, and then protest that they had been the faithful friends of the Colony.

In this case the result to the clans that followed Mapasa was most disastrous, for they met with very severe losses in the field, their principal leaders were killed, and the whole of them were reduced to utter destitution. At the close of the war Sir George Cathcart annexed to the Colony the Territory previously occupied by them, and termed it the Division of Queenstown. The scattered and impoverished Tembus he collected together and placed on a tract of land having the Indwe River as its eastern boundary, which tract of land was thenceforth known as the Tambookie Location, and has recently been formed into the Magisterial District of Glen Grey. Nonesi was invited to return from Tembuland Proper, and was appointed by Sir George Cathcart native head of the Location. This section of the Tembu tribe then lost its independence, for though the petty chiefs were still permitted to exercise authority over their people, and Nonesi was treated as their head, Mr. J. C. Warner was stationed in the Location as Government Agent, with supreme control over all.

In August 1864 the Imperial Government resolved to withdraw its authority from the country beyond the Indwe and the Kei which had been taken from Kreli in 1858. The Governor, Sir Philip Wodehouse, had previously intended to locate Europeans there, but as this plan was frustrated by the instructions of the Secretary of State, he had no choice left except as to what particular natives he should give the vacant country to. Under these circumstances in September 1864 he offered a portion of it to the Emigrant Tembus in exchange for the ground on the colonial side of the Indwe.* He had in view, first, the strengthening of the Tembu tribe as a counterpoise to the power of Kreli, and secondly, the acquisition of the land west of the Indwe for colonial purposes. The land which he offered in exchange for their Location was the tract of country between them and the rest of their tribe who were living in independence under the young chief Gangeli-zwe. It was separated from them only by the Indwe River, so that removal would be easy, and while even more fertile it was very much larger than the tract they were living on.

---

* A proposal to remove these Tembus to a part of the vacant country was made in general terms by Sir Philip Wodehouse in person to the chiefs when he visited the Location early in 1864. The details were left to be arranged after his departure. Meetings were then held, and the result was communicated to the Governor by Mr. J. C. Warner (then Agent with them) in the following terms:—

8th April, 1864.

"The Head Chiefs of the different Tribes have unanimously consented to remove on the following conditions:—

"That the boundaries of the future Tambookieland shall be from the source of the Indwe in the Wash bank range of mountains down the East bank of that river to its junction with the Kei, thence down the latter river to its junction with the Tsomo, thence up the West bank of the Tsomo to the waggon road at the Police Station, thence along the said waggon road to the Umgwali Drift below Clarkebury. Northern boundary the Wash bank and Quathlamba mountains.

"That this country be secured to them, and only to be forfeited in case of their making war on the Colony.

"That their independence be guaranteed to them as far as consistent with humanity and the paramount authority of the Queen.

"That their stipends be continued to them, and that they enjoy all the privileges they at present possess, and that the present Tambookie Agent shall be appointed as British Resident among them." †

---

† "They thus asked for a considerable portion of the territory now known as Fingoland, as well as the whole of the vacant country to the north. The Governor was not disposed to purchase the Tambookie Location at so dear a rate, but made the following

A lengthy correspondence ensued with Mr. Warner, who conducted the negotiations with the Tembus, and who was at first tolerably confident of being able to carry out the Governor's views. Matanzima, Darala, and Gecelo, the three most powerful chiefs in the Location, consented to the proposed exchange. For some months Sir Philip Wodehouse and Mr. Southey, then Colonial Secretary, seemed to hope for, if not to anticipate, success, their chief fear being that Nonesi would probably evade carrying out the plan in its entirety, by remaining behind herself with a few adherents. There was a strong feeling of jealousy between the old chieftainess and Raxoti (now called Matanzima), and it seemed likely that if one went the other would not. In this case the government (in February 1865) proposed to assign lands in the old Location sufficient for their purpose to Nonesi and such of her followers as should stay with her.

In the meantime a delay was caused by the request of the chiefs to be allowed time to gather their crops which were then growing. This was conceded as reasonable, but after the harvest there was no general movement. Sections of the people crossed the Indwe, though taking care always that a sufficient number should remain behind to prevent the occupation by any one else of the ground they were leaving. The Colonial Government was powerless in the matter. Force could not be used either to prevent a partial migration, or to drive the whole of the Tembus over the river. In June 1865 Mr. Warner announced that the scheme had completely broken down, and the Government could only regret that the announcement was true, remonstrate with the chiefs who remained in the old Location, strike off the salaries which they had previously drawn, and declare that henceforth they should be subject to Colonial law alone. In this manner the Tembus obtained possession of the whole of the upper portion of Kreli's former country, which has since that time been called Emigrant Tembuland, in addition to the Location granted to them by Sir George Cathcart, now known as the District of Glen Grey.

---

proposal: 'I have come to the conclusion that it is desirable that the Tambookies of the location, if they are to be moved at all, shall be moved quite to our eastern point,—that is to say to the east bank of the Tsomo ; and shall be allowed to occupy all the territory from the source of that river in the Stormberg down its left bank till nearly opposite the police station, and thence east by the wagon road to the Bashee.'" (Letter from Sir Philip Wodehouse to Mr. J. C. Warner, of 10th April 1864.)

The Governor's offer was thus to give only the country east of the Tsomo (much less than half of what is now known as Emigrant Tembuland) in exchange for the Tambookie Location. The district between the Tsomo and Indwe would have been reserved for colonization. The chiefs declined to accept this proposal, and it fell through sometime before the decision of the Secretary of State to abandon the country beyond the Indwe was known. These negotiations must not be confounded with those that followed after the receipt of the dispatch ordering the withdrawal of British dominion from the vacant territory, when Sir Philip Wodehouse had no option but to offer more than double the land that in April 1864 he proposed to give in exchange for the Tambookie Location.

The country beyond the Indwe was divided into four great blocks, over each of which there was a recognised chief. One of these was Matanzima, a brother of Gangelizwe; another was Darala, a descendant of Tembu, but a very distant relative of the paramount chief; the third and fourth were Gecelo, son of Tyopo, and Stokwe, son of Undlela, neither of whom were Tembus by descent. These chiefs and several others who were subordinate to them received yearly allowances from the Government. They were, however, treated as independent rulers. Their people paid no taxes to the Colonial Treasury, but a few European traders and woodcutters who went into the country paid licences to them. They governed their people and collected the isizi * and other dues from their subjects in the usual Kafir way.

A Diplomatic Agent, in the person of Mr. E. J. Warner, was stationed at Southeyville, to be the medium of communication with the Government. He was required to use his influence in controlling the relationship between the chiefs so as to preserve peace, but he had no other power than to recommend the stoppage of the annual allowances. The policy pursued towards the whole of the native people beyond the Colonial boundary was at that time, by direction of the Imperial Government, one of interfering with them as little as possible. There were intrigues and jealousies among the chiefs, and those who were not of Tembu descent were frequently quarrelling with Gangelizwe. On one of these occasions the Tembu Agent reported that a chief was sitting still and "trusted his conduct would meet with the approval of Government," to which the Colonial Secretary replied, "His Excellency does not feel himself justified to interfere in matters between foreign native headmen and the chief of their tribe."

On another occasion the Agent reported that he had been unable to arrange amicably a matter in dispute between Gecelo and Gangelizwe. The reply of the Colonial Secretary was: "I am directed to request that you will be so good as to state in what manner you deem it possible that this Government can effectually interfere in this matter without assuming to itself rights and power over a country and people which it does not possess." (10th January 1870).

Mr. Warner then asked for definite instructions, and received the following reply :—

7th March 1870. "I have submitted to His Excellency the High Commissioner your letter of the 11th ultimo requesting instructions as to the line of policy which should be observed in respect of the Emigrant Tambookies located in the Transkei Territory, particularly in relation to the attempted authority over them of which there are indications on the part of the chief Gangelizwe. His Excellency requests me to inform you that there can be no objection to your continuing to exercise a wholesome influence and

---

* "Isizi" means the fines paid to the chief for murder, assault, and other offences considered criminal, as distinguished from civil, in Kafir law. With some tribes, as for instance the Pondos, it also means an ox paid to the chief when the death of a man is reported by his relatives, to console him for the loss of a subject.

control over the people in question by all legitimate means, so far as they themselves are prepared to submit to your so doing. As regards Gangelizwe, that chief must be well aware that the Government does not recognise the slightest right on his part to exercise any authority over Emigrant Tambookies, but while you are authorised to guard against any admission of such pretensions, I am instructed to impress upon you that every care should be taken to avoid in this matter seeking out for causes of offence."

Early in 1872, however, the Government so far departed from its previous line of policy as to send a Commission to enquire into the disputes as to boundaries and to arbitrate between the contending chiefs. Certain lines were thereupon laid down, and were afterwards respected by all parties.

Mr. E. J. Warner was succeeded as Tembu Agent by Mr. William Fynn in May 1873, and Mr. Fynn was succeeded by Mr. Charles J. Levy in December 1875.

The chiefs who were least disposed to be guided by the advice of the Agent were Gecelo and Stokwe. The last named was a turbulent character, always ready for a quarrel with anybody. In August 1874 a dispute between these two chiefs ended in a battle between their clans, and there was danger of the surrounding natives being drawn into the vortex of strife. But by this time a change had taken place in the form of government of the Cape Colony, and the tone adopted towards disturbers of the peace was very different from what it had been four years earlier. The Government fined Gecelo and Stokwe each fifty head of cattle, and Mr. Brownlee, then Secretary for Native Affairs, addressed the Tembu Agent as follows:—

19th October 1874. "Government cannot allow the Emigrant Tambookie Location to be the arena for bloodshed, neither can the Emigrant Tambookies be allowed to pass by the Tambookie Agent and disregard his word. If war and bloodshed continue and the wishes of Government as expressed by you are disregarded, then Government will be necessitated to deal with the transgressors as it did with Kreli, and as they prove themselves unworthy of the kindness they have received from Government then others must be put into their place who will live in peace and regard and obey the orders of Government."

Early in 1877 Stokwe again showed a disposition to cause trouble, upon which Mr. Brownlee issued instructions that if he did not behave himself his allowance was to be reduced from £50 to £24 per annum, and his brother Matimbikati was to be made independent of him.

In the war of 1877-8 the Emigrant Tembus took no active part against the Colony, though it was known that the sympathies of many of them were with our enemies. On the 30th June, 1878, Gonya and Matanzima, two of the sons of the rebel Gaika chief Sandile, were captured by Mr. Levy at Stokwe Undlela's kraal, where they were found concealed in a hut. Some allowance, however, must be made for Stokwe in this case, as his great wife was a sister of the fugitive chiefs.

It is necessary now to turn to Tembuland Proper.

In 1863 Qeya, great son of Umtirara, was circumcised, when he took the name of Gangelizwe, and assumed the government of the Tembu tribe. On this occasion the Colonial authorities as a mark of friendship presented him with the sum of £50, and promised him an allowance of £52 a year. There had long been an ill feeling between the Tembus and Xosas, and this was now increased by personal jealousy between Gangelizwe and Sigcawu, great son of Kreli, who had also just come of age. Between the Tembus and the Fondos on the other side there was likewise a feud of long standing which now and again occasioned war. Under these circumstances, the influence of the late regent Joyi and the old councillors of Umtirara was in favour of keeping on good terms with the Colonial Government.

The Tembu tribe, as has been said before, waş not a compact body, inasmuch as many of its clans were of alien blood. The most powerful of Gangelizwe's vassals, indeed,—Dalasile, head of the Amaqwati clans,—was not a Tembu by descent, and was not inclined to admit much more than the precedence of the paramount ruler. He could bring almost as many followers into the field as Gangelizwe could from the kraals under his immediate government.

To strengthen himself, therefore, the young chief encouraged other aliens to settle in his country. He specially favoured a large Fingo clan under the chief Menziwe who had taken refuge in Tembuland in the time of Umtirara, and he induced a number of European farmers to settle along the western bank of the Umtata so as to form a barrier between him and the Pondos. A similar little European community was also formed at the Şlang River on another border of his territory. Each of these farmers paid him rent at the rate of £6 a year, and as by 1874 there were some eighty families settled in his country he derived a good income as well as some protection from them. In return he agreed to secure them against annoyance from his own subjects, but he failed to do so.

Gangelizwe was a man of savage disposition and ungovernable temper. In May 1866 he took as his great wife a daughter of the Xosa chief Kreli. The marriage was brought about by the councillors for political purposes, and affection had nothing to do with it. The treatment of this woman by her husband was so brutal that in 1870 she fled from him, and returned to her father maimed and covered with wounds. Fearing Kreli's vengeance, as soon as his wife left him the Tembu chief, through Mr. E. J. Warner, applied to the High Commissioner for an officer to reside with him, and a few months later repeated the request. Thereupon, in February 1871, Mr. E. B. Chalmers was appointed Resident with Gangelizwe, to advise him, and to be the medium of communication between him and the Government.

Acting by the advice of Mr. Fynn, who was then Resident with him, Kreli had submitted to the Government a complaint of the treatment of his daughter by Gangelizwe, and Messrs. Fynn and Chalmers were instructed to investigate the matter and report upon it. They did so, and in March 1871 the Governor pronounced judgment that Gangelizwe should pay to Kreli forty head of cattle. Kreli accepted the cattle awarded to him, though he considered the punishment altogether too slight. His people, incensed at the outrages inflicted on the chief's daughter, which they regarded as insults to themselves, and smarting under the occupation by the Emigrant Tembus of a tract of land that had once been theirs, were intent upon revenge. Plundering commenced, followed by retaliation, and presently the two tribes were practically at war.

On the 30th of September 1872, Kreli and his son Sigcawu crossed the Bashee at the head of a large army, and invaded Tembuland. As the Gcalekas advanced the Tembus fell back until the 6th of October when a great battle was fought in which the Tembus were totally defeated. Gangelizwe with his bodyguard fled to Clarkbury, a Wesleyan Mission Station which had been founded by the Rev. Mr. Haddy in 1830, and where the Rev. Mr. Hargreaves was then residing. This gentleman was possessed of a rare courage as well as enormous influence over the natives around him. He met Kreli, whose followers were elated with victory and half mad with excitement, and induced him to abstain from further pursuit.

Gangelizwe now offered to Mr. Chalmers to cede the whole of his country unconditionally to the British Government. The Resident asked that the offer should be made at a public meeting, and one was called for the purpose. On the 21st of October a number of the sub chiefs came together, and expressed a strong feeling in favour of the cession. Dalasile, however, and several others were not present.

A Commission consisting of Lieutenant-Colonel Edmondstone, of the 32nd Regiment, Mr. E. A. Judge, Civil Commissioner and Resident Magistrate of Queenstown, and Inspector J. Murray Grant, of the Frontier Armed and Mounted Police, was sent to the scene of disturbances and succeeded in inducing Kreli to suspend hostilities. When this was settled, the Commission was informed by Gangelizwe, at a meeting which took place on the 30th of November 1872, that his offer of his country and his people to the Government had been made without sufficient consideration and without the consent of some of his principal subordinate chiefs, and that as there was considerable opposition to its being carried out he wished to withdraw it. As afterwards ascertained, it was Dalasile who overruled the proposal of Gangelizwe to come under the Government.

Mr. Brownlee, Secretary for Native Affairs, then visited the Gcaleka and Tembu country. On the 20th of January 1873 he met Kreli, who had six thousand warriors with him, and persuaded him to send four delegates to Idutywa to meet Gangelizwe's representatives. The Tembu Chief gladly sent the same number of delegates, and Mr. Brownlee was able to induce them to make a formal declaration of peace.

In May 1873 Mr. Chalmers was succeeded as Resident with Gangelizwe by Mr. William Wright.

In 1875 Gangelizwe's conduct brought the tribe again into imminent danger of war. Among his concubines there was a Gcaleka woman, an illegitimate niece of Kreli, who had accompanied the great wife as an attendant when she went to Tembuland, and remained there ever since. Gangelizwe in a fit of passion inflicted very severe injuries upon this woman, and two days later ordered a young man named Ndevu to break her skull with a kerrie. The murder was committed on the 25th of July. On the 27th the Chief's messenger reported at the residency that the woman had been four days ill with headache and pain in the side. On the 29th Mr. Wright was informed that she had died. For some months previous to the murder it was known that the woman was undergoing brutal treatment, and once it was rumoured that she was dead. Kreli then sent messengers to request that she might be allowed to visit her relatives, but the Resident could not induce Gangelizwe either to consent to this or to permit the messengers to see her.

Gangelizwe's residence, where the murder was committed, was in the neighbourhood of the ground occupied by the Fingo chief, Menziwe. That chief, apprehending that war with the Gcalekas would be the immediate consequence, declared publicly that he would remain neutral. This declaration so irritated Gangelizwe that he prepared to attack Menziwe, who thereupon fled with his people to Idutywa and requested protection from Mr. J. H. Garner, who during Mr. Cumming's absence in Griqualand East was acting there as Superintendent. On the 5th of August Menziwe's women and cattle crossed the Bashee into the Idutywa, and were followed by the warriors of the clan, six hundred in number, who were pursued to the river's edge by a Tembu army.

Kreli was induced on this occasion, as at the time of his daughter's ill treatment, to refer the matter to the Government, and the residents with the two chiefs, Messrs. J. Ayliff and W. Wright, were instructed to hold an investigation. The inquiry took place at Idutywa, in the presence of four representatives sent by each of the chiefs. Umbande, son of Menziwe, who had been one of Gangelizwe's most confidential advisers, was the principal witness. After taking evidence, Messrs. Ayliff and Wright found there was no question of Gangelizwe's guilt, whereupon the Governor inflicted upon him a fine of two hundred head of cattle and £100 in money.

If the murdered woman had been a Tembu probably nothing more would have been heard of the matter. But she was a Gcaleka, and the people of her tribe, who were not satisfied with Gangelizwe's punishment, seemed resolved to avenge her death. Commandant Bowker was therefore instructed to enter Tembuland with a strong body of the Frontier Police, reinstate Menziwe, the Fingo chief whom Gangelizwe had driven away, and prevent hostilities by the Gcalekas. On the 14th of September the Police crossed the Bashee for this purpose with Menziwe's clan.

Gangelizwe and his subordinate chiefs then did as they had done once before in a time of difficulty: they offered to place their country and their tribe under the control of the Government. On the 28th of October 1875 the terms of the cession, as drawn up in writing by the

Rev. Mr. Hargreaves on behalf of the Tembus, were discussed with Commandant Bowker and Mr. Wright at a meeting held at Clarkbury, at which all the chiefs of note in Tembuland Proper except Dalasile, were present.

The Tembus proposed that Gangelizwe and fourteen heads of clans, who were named should be recognised by the Government as chiefs, and that salaries, the amounts of which were mentioned, should be paid to them; that no hut tax should be payable until 1878; that the boundaries of the country should be made as previously fixed; that the chiefs should retain judicial authority over their people, except in cases of certain specified crimes, and subject to appeal to Magistrates; that the government of the Mission Stations should not be interfered with; that the Fingo chief Menziwe should be removed to a locality which was named; and that the sale of spirituous liquors to natives should be prohibited. These proposals were forwarded to the Government, and were agreed to, with the sole exception that Gangelizwe could not be recognised as a chief, though a salary of £200 would be paid to him yearly.

On the 10th of December another meeting of the chiefs and people took place at Emjanyana, when Commandant Bowker announced officially that the country and people had been taken over on the above terms, and that Mr. S. A. Probart would shortly be sent as a Special Commissioner to conclude the arrangements. At this meeting proposals were made on behalf of Dalasile, to come under the Government, and were agreed to by Commandant Bowker. The conditions were that his people should not be mixed with others, but should have a separate magistrate; that he should receive a salary of £100 a year; and a few others similar to those under which Gangelizwe's immediate adherents were taken over.

A few days later Mr. Probart, who was then a member of the Legislative Assembly, arrived in Tembuland. On the 24th of December he announced at a great meeting at Emjanyana that the Government had ratified everything that Commandant Bowker had done. The conditions of the cession, as proposed by the Tembu chiefs, were agreed to, except that Gangelizwe must be deprived of all authority; but the Commissioner added that it would depend upon the manner in which he should conduct himself whether at some future time he might not be entrusted by the Government with power in his own section of the tribe.

Dalasile was not present at this meeting, but on the 31st Mr. Probart met him at All Saint's Mission, informed him that the agreement made between him and Commandant Bowker was ratified, and asked him if he and his people were still of the same mind as to coming under Government. Dalasile requested to be allowed an hour for consideration. After consultation with his councillors, he then explained that what he desired was that he should come under Government himself, but retain the sole control of his people. All complaints, he thought, should be made to him, and the magistrate should have only joint power of settlement. Mr. Probart explained that this was not the meaning of the conditions agreed to, and after some argument Dalasile promised to adhere to his original proposals. That from the very first, however, this chief had no real intention of surrendering any power is shown by the circumstance that he never drew the salary to which he was entitled under the conditions of cession.

In this manner Tembuland Proper became a portion of the British dominions. The Special Commissioner submitted proposals to the Government for the division of the country into judicial districts, which were acted upon at once, and in 1876 the four magistracies of Emja-nyana, Engcobo, Umtata, and Mqanduli were created.

The first of these, Emjanyana, was the residence of the former Agent, Mr. Wright, and he was left there as Magistrate with the additional title and authority of Chief Magistrate of Tembuland Proper.

The second, Engcobo, was the site selected for the magistrate with Dalasile's people. In April Mr. W. E. Stanford was stationed there as magistrate.

In the third, Umtata, the seat of magistracy has recently become the most important town in Kafirland. Major J. F. Boyes assumed duty as Magistrate there in the month of April.

The fourth district, Mqanduli, occupies the lower portion of Tembu-land Proper. In August the Rev. John H. Scott was stationed there as magistrate.

The European farmers in the country remained on the same condi-tions as before, except that they were required to pay the annual rent to the Government instead of to Gangelizwe.

It was soon discovered that the power of Gangelizwe could not easily be set aside. The Government, the magistrates, and some of the alien clans might ignore him, but the clans of pure Tembu blood would not. All their national traditions, their ideas of patriotism, their feelings of pride, prompted them to be loyal to him. Stronger still than any of these motives was their religion. The belief of the Kafir is firm that the spirits of the dead chiefs hold the destinies of the tribes in their keeping. To renounce allegiance to the Chief, the descendant and representative of those to whose spirits they offer sacrifices and whose wrath they dread as the greatest calamity that can overtake them, is in the Kafir way of thinking the most enormous of crimes. Our magistrates encountered such difficulty in governing the people, owing to their sullen demeanour and continual complaints of the degradation to which their chief was subjected, that at the close of 1876 it was considered necessary to restore Gangelizwe to his former rank and to treat him as the highest native official in the country.

When the war with Kreli began in 1877, Major Elliot, who in August of that year succeeded Mr. Wright as Chief Magistrate, called upon the Tembus to take up arms for the Government. In the district of Mqanduli, the Magistrate, Mr. Scott, succeeded in raising a native force of some strength, but in the other districts there was no response to the call to arms. Not a single individual of any clan under Dalasile came forward to aid the Government. Stokwe son of Tyali who resided in Maxongo's Hoek at the base of the Drakensberg, joined the enemy. He was the head of a small alien clan called the Amavundle. All the rest of the tribe waited for the word of Gangelizwe. Fortunately, that chief had sufficient sagacity to see that an opportunity had occurred for him to secure the favour of the Government. He declared himself a loyal subject, and took the field with Major Elliot. At once, as if by magic, the attitude of the people changed. From all sides they came in to join their chief, and thereafter rendered valuable assistance.

Dalasile was fined a hundred head of cattle for not complying with the orders of the Chief Magistrate. Stokwe Tyali was assisted by Umfanta and a body of rebels from the Queenstown Division, but in March 1878 Major Elliot fell upon him with a combined burgher and native force, routed him after a sharp engagement, seized his cattle, and drove him and his adherents out of Maxongo's Hoek. He and Umfanta were both made prisoners in the following month.

At the close of the war of 1877-8 the Government resolved to make several important changes in the administration of the native territories. The staff of sub-magistrates was to be increased, and the people were to be brought more under their jurisdiction. To secure a greater degree of uniformity in the systems of management, various districts which had been previously under separate heads were to be united under the same Chief Magistrate.

Emigrant Tembuland was divided into two judicial districts, named Southeyville and Xalanga. Mr. C. J. Levey, who had previously borne the title of Tembu Agent, was henceforth termed magistrate of Southeyville, and in July 1878 Mr. Wm. G. Cumming assumed duty as Assistant Magistrate at Xalanga.

The Hon. Wm. Ayliff, then Secretary for Native Affairs, made a tour through Kafirland for the purpose of explaining the new system to the people and obtaining their consent to its introduction. On the 16th of September 1878 he met the Emigrant Tembu chiefs Matanzima, Darala, Gecelo and Stokwe at Cofimvaba, and after some discussion obtained their consent to the payment of hut tax. He informed them that over the ordinary magistrate there would be an officer to whom they could appeal whenever they thought justice was not done to them by the lower courts. The chiefs, according to native custom, thanked Mr. Ayliff for the information, and appeared to be satisfied.

The arrangement thus indicated was carried out by the union of Emigrant Tembuland and Tembuland Proper under Major Elliot as Chief Magistrate. In December 1878 Major Elliot paid his first visit to the territory thus added to that previously under his charge. He found the chiefs discontented and half defiant. They told him that they had been promised when they moved from the old Tambookie Location that they would be regarded as independent in the country over the Indwe, and now they were being made subject to magistrates, much against their will. Major Elliot replied that they had no cause to complain, as by leaving people behind their section of the tribe had secured both countries.

In 1879 hut tax was first paid in the united territories of Emigrant Tembuland and Tembuland Proper. Before that date the Colony had borne the expense of maintaining establishments without deriving any direct revenue from the people, except a trifling amount from the few European traders and farmers in Tembuland Proper.

The third section of this Chief Magistracy is Bomvanaland, a small tract of country on the sea coast eastward of the Bashee. The Bomvanas are part of a tribe that was dispersed in the convulsions of the early part of the present century. Another section of the same tribe is called Amatshesi, and is at the present time residing partly in Pondoland and partly in Tembuland. The Bomvana section, under the chief Gambushe, grandfather of Moni, when driven out of Pondoland applied to the Gcaleka chief Kawuta to be received as a vassal clan, and was located by him along the Bashee. Subsequently they moved deeper into Gcalekaland, but in 1857 they decided not to destroy their cattle and grain as Kreli's people were then doing, and therefore retreated to the country in which they have since been residing.

It was with the Bomvanas, then under the chief Moni, that Kreli took refuge when driven from his own country in 1858. Though they had refused to follow the Gcalekas in the course which led to their dispersion, Moni and his clan were faithful to them in their distress, and gave them all the succour that was in their power to bestow. In 1877 the Government placed a Resident with Moni, in the person of Mr. Wm. Fynn, who assumed duty on the 30th of June in that year. The clan was still, however, considered as in a condition of vassalage to the Gcaleka chief.

When the war of 1877 commenced, Moni announced his intention of remaining neutral. He did not attempt to conceal his attachment to Kreli, and stated that he would not abandon him in any ordinary peril, but to resist the Government was hopeless. When the Gcalekas fled across the Bashee before Colonel Griffith, some of them took refuge with the Pondos, but most retreated no further than Bomvanaland. As the war extended, it became necessary to close this district against the enemy, and Major Elliot was instructed by Sir Bartle Frere to place himself in communication with Moni and take such further steps as the Commander of the Forces might direct.

On the 7th of January 1878 Major Elliot had an interview at Moni's residence with the chief and the principal men of the Bomvana clan. Moni himself was at this time believed to be over eighty years of age, he was blind and too feeble to travel, but his mental faculties were perfect. Mr. Arthur Stanford and Mr. William Fynn were present at the interview and acted as interpreters. Major Elliot explained that the Bomvanas were too weak to remain independent and neutral in such a struggle as that going on, they were unable to prevent the Gcalekas from making use of their country as a place of shelter and base of operations, and therefore it was necessary for the Government to take military occupation of it and hold it during the war. To this no objection was made, as in the nature of things it was not a proposal but an announcement.

A few days later Moni sent his son Langa and his principal councillors to Mr. Fynn with a request that he would forward to Government the following message: "I wish to become a British subject. I
place my tribe and country under the Government, and I now ask the
Government to send Colonel Eustace to assist my magistrate in
making arrangements for taking over the Bomvana tribe."

Colonel Eustace was accordingly directed to proceed to Bomvanaland, and on the 28th of February 1878 he and Major Elliot reached the
chief's residence. A meeting was at once held, at which Moni, his
sons, councillors, sub-chiefs, and about three hundred of his people were
present. Mr. Wm. Fynn, the Resident, acted as interpreter. Colonel
Eustace addressed the chiefs and people to the effect that he had come
at *their* request, that the Government had no wish to deprive them of
their independence, that if they became British subjects it would be of
their own free will, that they would then have to pay tax and
accept magistrates, and that the chiefs would have to relinquish
nearly all their power and influence. They replied that they wished to
come under Government upon the same conditions as were agreed to
in the case of the Tembus. Colonel Eustace then accepted them
formally as British subjects. After this had been done, Moni said he
hoped annual allowances would be granted to himself and several other
chiefs whom he named. This Colonel Eustace promised to recommend.

Mr. Fynn, the previous Resident, was henceforth styled magistrate,
and exercised judicial powers. It was not until December 1878 that
Bomvanaland was attached to the Chief Magistracy of Tembuland. In
1880 the Bomvanas first paid hut tax. These people have as yet hardly
been affected, even in outward appearance, by European civilization.
The chief Moni is still living, though helpless with extreme age, and his
son Langa is regarded by the Bomvanas as their head. There are
many refugee Gcalekas in the district, Kreli having taken up his
residence there after the war, and having been left there undisturbed
by the Government. Between the Bomvanas and the Tembus there
has never been a good feeling.

The Amatshesi, though of the same tribe, have long been at variance
with the Bomvana branch. Makunzi, their chief, became a vassal of
the Tembus when he crossed the Umtata fifty or sixty years ago.
Some of these people occupy the country along the coast between
Bomvanaland and the Umtata, others are living in Pondoland. Pali,
their present chief, succeeded his father Makunzi. His position seems
to be a peculiar one. The country in which he lives, as far as the
Umtata, is British territory under the cession by the Tembus, but the
Amatshesi have not been placed under the jurisdiction of a magistrate.
Makunzi requested to be received as a British subject, but was advised
by Mr. Probart to withdraw his application. Pali has repeatedly made
the same request, and the magistrate of Mqanduli has more than once
urged that something should be done in the matter. The difficulty
seems to be that part of the clan is in Pondoland and that Pali himself
is not likely to make an obedient subject. He is supposed to have
about four hundred fighting men on this side of the Umtata.

The year 1880 was one of unrest in Tembuland. In the early months the air was full of rumours of a combination among the native tribes to throw off the supremacy of the white man. It was impossible for the magistrates to ascertain what was taking place, what plans were being concerted, or where the explosion would likely be felt first, but all were agreed that there were very grave reasons for uneasiness. In October this state of uncertainty was brought to an end by Umhlonhlo's murder of the magistrate and two other Europeans at Qumbu in the adjoining province of Griqualand East. This was the signal for rebellion in Tembuland, and immediately several of the clans rose in arms.

Without delay Major Elliot issued instructions to all the magistrates in the territory to collect the Europeans and other loyal inhabitants of their districts, and to retire either to the Colony or to Umtata, whichever could be reached with greater chance of safety. Umtata was the only place he thought of holding. In his instructions he pointed out that nothing could cause greater anxiety to the Government, or tend more to impede prompt military operations, than the necessity of providing columns for the relief of small detached positions of no strategical importance which were not provisioned or in other respects prepared to stand a siege. Most of the outlying magistracies were thereupon abandoned. Mr. Levey, who believed that he could defend Southeyville, remained at his post until a burgher force arrived with instructions to rescue him and then leave the place to its fate. As soon as this was carried out the office and residency were plundered and burnt by rebels.

The clans that took up arms against the Government were the Amaqwati under Dalasile, occupying the district of Engcobo in Tembuland Proper, and those under the chiefs Gecelo and Stokwe Ndlela in Emigrant Tembuland. Among these there were no Tembus by descent except a few men who followed Siqungati, a brother of Gangelizwe. Another alien clan which had come into Emigrant Tembuland a few years before, under the petty chief Kosana, went into rebellion, though Kosana himself remained loyal and took service with the Colonial forces. All eyes were now turned towards Gangelizwe, for upon him alone it rested whether the rebellion should become general or not. He decided, as before, to be faithful to the Government, and after this announcement was strengthened by his action in joining the Chief Magistrate, not a single clan rose against us, though the sympathies of the whole people were known to be entirely with the rebels.

It thus became a comparatively easy matter to suppress the insurrection. The districts occupied by the rebels were swept by the colonial forces. By February 1881 the insurrection was at an end, for the rebels had lost everything, had been driven out of their country and were thoroughly subdued.

In the session of 1882 the Cape Parliament referred to a Select Committee the question of the future occupation of the lands taken from the rebels. This Committee brought up a report recommending that the portion of Emigrant Tembuland formerly occupied by the chief Gecelo should be allotted to European farmers; that the consent of the Imperial Government should be obtained for the issue of titles, in case annexation to the Colony should be delyaed; that the remaining lands taken from rebels in Emigrant Tembuland should be granted under individual tenure to natives, irrespective of the tribal relationships; that as Dalasile's district belonged to the Tembu tribe it should not be occupied without the approval of the paramount chief Gangelizwe, but that steps should be taken to obtain his consent to its occupation by European farmers; and that a Commission should be appointed without delay to deal with the matter on these lines. The House of Assembly hereupon expressed its opinion in favour of the appointment of such a Commission as that referred to, and the Governor carried the resolution into effect.

The Tembuland Commission consisted of Messrs. J. Hemming, Civil Commissioner and Resident Magistrate of Queenstown, J. J. Irvine and J. L. Bradfield, members of the House of Assembly, and C. J. Bekker, Justice of the Peace for the District of Wodehouse, appointed on the 17th of August 1882, and Messrs. J. J. Janse van Rensberg and J. Joubert, members of the House of Assembly, appointed on the 22nd of September following.

In the meantime portions of the vacant territory had been taken possession of by Europeans from the Colony who went in without leave, but subsequently made no objection to paying grazing licences to the Government. The conflicting claims advanced by these people and their friends, by missionary societies, by traders, by chiefs and people, loyal, neutral, and late rebels, made the task of the Commission an extremely difficult one. Gangelizwe was the least troublesome of all to deal with. He made a formal cession of the northern parts of the district of Engcobo, and sent four of his councillors to point out the boundary between it and the part which he reserved for his own people. In Emigrant Tembuland a line between Europeans and Natives was laid down, against which Messrs. Bekker, van Rensberg, and Joubert protested as giving an undue proportion to the latter, but it has been maintained, and the country below it has been filled up with natives of different tribes, in the manner recommended by the Parliamentary Committee.

The land assigned for occupation by Europeans lies along the base of the Drankensberg between the Division of Wodehouse and Griqualand East. Its whole extent, including the Slang River settlement which dates from 1867, is only seven hundred and twelve square miles, and from this must be deducted thirty-eight square miles occupied as a native location in Maxongo's Hoek.

The late rebels were located chiefly in the centre of Emigrant Tembuland in a magisterial district called Cala, formed of parts of the former district of Southeyville and Xalanga. Mr. C. Levey was stationed there as magistrate. The remainder of the district of Southeyville, or the portion occupied by the clans under Matanzima and Darala, was formed into a separate district, called St. Mark's, and in May 1881 Mr. R. W. Stanford assumed duty there as magistrate. Emigrant Tembuland was thus divided into three magisterial districts, St. Mark's and Cala occupied by natives, and Xalanga occupied by

Europeans. In September 1884 these three districts were again formed into two, by the partition of Cala between Xalanga and St. Mark's. Mr. Levey thereupon became magistrate of Xalanga. In May 1884 Mr. R. W. Stanford was succeeded at St. Mark's by Mr. T. R. Merriman, who remained when the district was enlarged.

In 1882 part of an abandoned tract of land along the Umtata, on which European farmers had been located by Gangelizwe before the cession of the country, was purchased from that chief by the Government, for the purpose of providing commonage for a town which was becoming a place of importance. The site is a central one for the whole of the native territories between the Kei and Natal. The town of Umtata is situated on the western bank of the river of the same name, and is two thousand two hundred feet above the level of the sea. Across the river Pondoland stretches away; and to the north-west, in Griqualand East, the Matiwane Mountains, clad with forests, rise full in view. The water of the river has not yet been led into the town, but already a good many trees have been planted. Umtata has become an important commercial centre, is a military station, and is the residence of the Bishop of Kaffraria. It now (December 1884) contains 140 buildings, many of which, however, are only structures of iron. Among them are the Court House and Public Offices (of stone), an English cathedral (of iron), a second English Church, a Roman Catholic Mission Church, a Wesleyan Church, a Theatre, and several large stores. The European population, exclusive of the Colonial military forces, numbers four hundred and ninety souls.

No portion of the Chief Magistracy of Tembuland has yet been annexed to the Cape Colony. On the 22nd of June 1876 the House of Assembly upon the motion of the Colonial Secretary, seconded by Mr. Stigant resolved that "It is expedient that the country . . . . known as Tembuland should be annexed to this colony and that the Government take such steps as may place it in a position to introduce a Bill to effect such annexation." On the 30th of July 1878 a similar resolution was carried with respect to Bomvanaland. The delay in obtaining the sanction of the Imperial Government, the passing in 1880 of an Annexation Act by the Cape Parliament, the failure of the Act on account of its not receiving the Royal assent within the requisite time, and the resolution of the Cape Parliament in 1884 reaffirming the expediency of annexing the territory, were all influenced by the same causes as were in operation in the case of Gcalekaland, and followed precisely the same course.

The Chief Magistracy is ruled by the Governor of the Cape Colony under a special Commission whereby he is appointed "Governor of certain territories . . . . commonly known as Tembuland, Emigrant Tambookieland, Bomvanaland and Gcalekaland, and now part of Her Majesty's Dominions." Practically the Government is carried on through the native office. The regulations in force were published by proclamation on the 26th of January 1882, and are the same as those of Gcalekaland.

Under the conditions of cession, the chiefs have power to try all civil and all petty criminal cases. From their decisions appeals can be made to the magistrate, or suitors may bring their cases before the magistrate in the first instance if they chose to do so. Important criminal cases are tried by a court of three magistrates with the Chief Magistrate as President. Native law is carried out in cases where natives only are concerned. No one in Tembuland is allowed to sell spirituous liquor to natives, under penalty of a fine of £50 and being disqualified to trade thereafter in the territory. On the recommendation of the magistrate of a district, the Chief Magistrate may grant a licence to sell spirits to Europeans only. The population of the Chief Magistracy must be considerably in excess of one hundred thousand, bnt no reliable figures can be given. According to the census of 1879 there were 98,410 souls in the territory, but that was before the disturbances. The natives consist (a) of Tembus, who form a majority, (b) of Fingos, who have been crowding in of late years in considerable numbers, (c) of Bomvanas, (d) of Refugee Gcalekas, (e) of Amatshesi, (f) of the mixed races—Gaikas, Bastards, &c.,—recently located in Emigrant Tembuland.

On the 31st of December 1884 the chief Gangelizwe died. His son by the great wife, Dalindyebo, who is now regarded by the Tembus as their head, is only eighteen years of age. He is a grandson of the Gcaleka chief Kreli. In June the Emigrant Tembu chief Darala died. His great son being too young to succeed him, the clan is at present under the control of a regent.

The Colonial Government has at present (exclusive of military and police) twenty-two European officials in Tembuland, viz., one Chief Magistrate, seven sub-magistrates, one accountant, ten clerks, and three district surgeons.

The Chief Magistrate is Major H. G. Elliot.

The sub-magistrates of the several districts since their establishment have been:—

Emigrant Tembuland:

XALANGA:	Mr. C. J. Levey.
ST. MARK'S:	Mr. T. R. Merriman.

Tembuland Proper:

ENGCOBO:	Mr. W. E. Stanford.
EMJANYANA:	Major J. F. Boyes, September, 1878.
	Mr. M. B. Shaw, January, 1883.
	Mr. H. S. Vice, October, 1884.
UMTATA:	Major J. F. Boyes.
	Mr. A. H. B. Stanford, September, 1878.
MQANDULI:	Rev. J. H. Scott.
	Mr. C. F. Blakeway, August, 1878.

Bomvanaland:

ELLIOTDALE:	Mr. Wm. Fynn.
	Mr. H. S. Vice (Acting), January, 1879.
	Mr. J. T. O'Connor, May 1880.
	Mr. H. S. Vice (Acting), December, 1881.
	Mr. J. W. Morris, July, 1883.

The revenue collected in the Chief Magistracy of Tembuland from the 1st of July 1879 to the 31st of December 1883 was £68,337 0s. 5d., and the expenditure for civil purposes during the same period was £147,683 19s. 5d., or £79,346 19s. more than the revenue. Schools received £21,148 1s. 4d., or 31 per cent. of the revenue.

From the 1st of January to the 31st of December 1884 the receipts were £18,398 17s. 1d.,   Of this amount, Land (Hut Tax and Quitrent) contributed £12,896 4s. 1d., Licences £2165 9s. 2d. Fines, Forfeitures, &c., £1649 9s. 2d., Stamps £548 11s. 4d., Transfer Dues £273 8s., Telegraph Receipts £269 14s. 11d., and Miscellaneous Receipts £596 0s. 5d.

The expenditure for civil purposes in the Chief Magistracy of Tembuland during the year ending the 31st December 1884 was as follows:—

	£	s.	d.
Ordinary Expenditure	17,621	11	0
Education	4,660	2	2
Stationery	82	10	8
Survey Expenses	5,431	19	0
Telegraphs	449	13	0
Post Offices	1,521	1	7
	£29,766	17	5

In addition, there is a small sum for public works. One large item of expenditure, £5431 19s. is for a special service, and the reductions have been so recently made that there is not yet time for a large diminution of the expenses to be apparent. It is confidently anticipated that the revenue and expenditure during the current year will balance each other.   The educational grants are still at the rate of twenty-five per cent. of the revenue.

Genealogical Table showing the relationship of the Tembu chiefs:—

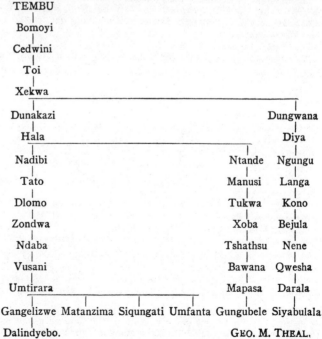

TEMBU
|
Bomoyi
|
Cedwini
|
Toi
|
Xekwa
|
Dunakazi   Dungwana
| |
Hala   Diya
| | |
Nadibi   Ntande   Ngungu
| | |
Tato   Manusi   Langa
| | |
Dlomo   Tukwa   Kono
| | |
Zondwa   Xoba   Bejula
| | |
Ndaba   Tshathsu   Nene
| | |
Vusani   Bawana   Qwesha
| | |
Umtirara   Mapasa   Darala
| | | | | | |
Gangelizwe Matanzima Siqungati Umfanta Gungubele Siyabulala

Dalindyebo.   GEO. M. THEAL.

GRIQUALAND EAST AND MOUNT AYLIFF.

(BLUE BOOK ON NATIVE AFFAIRS 1885).

The Chief Magistracy of Griqualand East is a tract of country in the form of an irregular parallelogram, about seven thousand two hundred and forty square miles in extent, occupying the plateau along the seaward base of the Quathlamba * or Drakensberg range. It is bounded on the northwest by Basutoland and the District of Barkly, from which it is separated by the Quathlamba; on the southwest by Tembuland, the dividing line being the head waters of the Umtata river and the watershed between the streams which flow into the Bashee and the Umzimvubu; on the southeast by Pondoland and the County of Alfred in Natal, a well defined boundary having been beaconed off; and on the northeast by the Colony of Natal, the Indwana, Ingwangwani, and Umzimkulu rivers marking the division on this side. No part of the territory is nearer the sea than thirty miles in a straight line.

The soil of Griqualand East is in general fertile and covered with a rich carpeting of grass. Horses and horned cattle thrive as well as in the most favoured parts of South Africa, and the pasturage along the slopes of the Drakensberg is particularly well adapted for sheep. Wheat grows in perfection, as does nearly every fruit, grain and vegetable of the warmer part of the temperate zone. The lowest section of the territory, a depression on the side nearest the sea, has an elevation of not less than three thousand feet above the ocean. From this depression there is a constant upward incline until the great mountain wall is reached. The most elevated portions of Griqualand East are therefore so cold in winter that the natives have never cared to occupy them. Europeans find the climate as pleasant and healthy as any in the world, though, owing probably to the air being damper, chest diseases are more common than on the great plains of the interior. In the summer months, when the prevailing winds are from the ocean and when thunder storms gather along the mountains, the rainfall is usually considerable; but there are occasional seasons of drought, never, however, equalling in duration those sometimes experienced in districts to the westward. Upon the whole this territory is considered capable of supporting a denser population than any other tract of land of equal area in the Cape Colony.

Our ownership of Griqualand East is based nominally on a cession made by the Pondo chief Faku, in reality it rests on the right of a civilized power to enforce order in districts occupied by barbarians. Faku never had any authority in it, he never would have had a claim to a rood of its soil if such claim had not been given to him by a treaty with a Colonial Governor. This treaty was made in 1844 by Sir Peregrine Maitland, with a view of securing an ally in the rear of the frontier Kafirs. At that time hardly anything was known by the

---

* More correctly Kahlamba. There is no click in the word, such as is signified by the letter q in native names. But long usage by writers and mapmakers has established the spelling as Quathlamba.

Colonial Government of the political condition of the natives in the valley of the Umzimvubu. Along the lower course of the river the Pondo tribe was found by travellers and missionaries, and it was assumed that the whole region was under the jurisdiction of Faku, the Pondo chief.

Faku was not slow in perceiving the advantages to be derived from an alliance with the Colony. Tshaka and Dingaan were dead, and the terrible Zulu power had been shattered, but he had many enemies still. A powerful friend at a safe distance was most desirable. He therefore accepted without hesitation the proposals made to him by Sir Peregrine Maitland's agents, and affixed his mark to a treaty, in the twelfth clause of which he was acknowledged as paramount chief of the whole region between the Umtata and the Umzimkulu, from the Drakensberg to the sea. In the thirteenth clause the Government undertook to secure this territory to him against British subjects, but the rights of all petty chiefs, and native tribes residing in any part of it were to remain unaltered. As since ascertained, the population of the country between the Umtata and the Umzimkulu at that time consisted of:—

(a) The Pondo tribe, occupying the banks of the Umzimvubu for forty or fifty miles upwards from the sea. These Pondos had lived there as long as their tradition went back, and though Zulu armies had swept off their stock and reduced them to great destitution, they had managed to preserve their lives by retiring into mountain recesses and thickly wooded ravines till the waves of invasion rolled over. In 1844 Faku was paramount chief of this tribe and directly governed the eastern clans, while Ndamase, his eldest son of the right hand house, ruled the clans on the western side of the river. Umqikela, the eldest son of the great house and consequently the heir to the paramount chieftainship, was still a youth.

(b) The Pondomisi tribe, living eastward of the Umtata, further inland than the Pondos. This tribe, as far back as could be traced, had always been independent, and had occupied nearly the same position as it did in 1844. It was divided into two rival sections, so well known in later times as those of the chiefs Umhlonhlo and Umditshwa.

(c) The Bacas under the chief Ncapayi, who was then acting as regent during the minority of his brother. These people were the remnant of a northern tribe which had suffered greatly in the wars of Tshaka, and when driven from their own country had fled to the district they were occupying in 1844. Hereditary right to the ground there they had of course none, but their claim to it was as good as could be set up by anyone else. These people have since broken up into several clans, one of which is now under Nomtsheketshe, their chief of highest hereditary rank, another is under Makaula, a son of Ncapayi, and some living on the Natal border look up to Mr. Donald Strachan as their head.

(d) The Xesibes, the remnant of a tribe that some eight generations earlier had migrated from the northern part of the present Colony of

Natal and settled in a district near that in which they are still living. Tshaka drove them beyond the Umtata, but after his death they returned. The whole country had been in commotion, and there was hardly a clan in it that had not been displaced. The Xesibes, on recrossing the Umzimvubu, lived for a time a nomadic life, but at length took possession of a tract of land to which the Amanci clan of the Pondos had a claim, and thus was originated a feud that exists to this day. These are the people of the chief Jojo.

(e) A great number of little groups of refugees with different titles, an enumeration of which would only cause confusion. The Pondos, owing largely to the prestige gained by their alliance with the Colony, have managed since that time to incorporate most of these clans. They are principally offshoots of the great tribe of the Abambo, who once occupied the coast region of Natal.

(f) Various refugee clans occupying the tract of land between the Umtamvuna and Umzimkulu rivers. These need not be further alluded to here, as with their district they were in after years annexed to the Colony of Natal.

(g) A number of Bushmen roaming over the otherwise uninhabited region along the base of the Drakensberg.

Among these various tribes and clans war was perpetually carried on. Somebody was always fancying the cattle or the cornfields of somebody else, or keeping alive ancient feuds by burning villages and slaughtering opponents. Combinations among the various sections of the community were continually changing, so that it is not only wearisome to follow them through their quarrels, but it can serve no good purpose to do so. The Pondos were the strongest of any one party, but they could not reduce the Pondomise, the Bacas or the Xesibes to subjection. As for Faku, he gained the reputation, which he kept to the day of his death, of being a faithful ally of the Colonial Government, which being interpreted means that he was always ready to fall upon the frontier Kafirs when we were at war with them, and stock his kraals with cattle at their expense.

In one respect the Maitland treaty pressed heavily upon the Pondo chief. The Natal Government maintained that as he was the paramount ruler of the whole country along their south-western border, he was bound to prevent stocklifting by his subjects, and when the Bushmen of the uplands committed depredations he was held responsible and compelled to make good the loss. In 1850 his nominal dignity cost him in this way a thousand head of cattle, the whole spoil of a raid upon his neighbour's kraals. Naturally this irritated him, and while smarting under the loss of his oxen he sent word to Maritzburg that he had not asked for the upper country, Government had forced it on him, and rather than be held accountable for the misdeeds of its inhabitants he would prefer to see Government taking possession and directly ruling it. Shortly afterwards, when the Lieutenant-Governor restored six hundred of the cattle and the remembrance of the penalty attached to his dignity was less distinct, he retracted this message; but from that time forward it was admitted that the twelfth clause of the Maitland treaty could not be carried out.

Sir George Grey looked upon the tract along the base of the Drakensberg as waste land at his disposal as the highest authority in South Africa. After the war between the Basutos and the Free State in 1858, he was desirous of locating there some of the restless clans whose presence on the Basuto frontier was a permanent hindrance to the establishment of order. His plan was, however, frustrated by an exceedingly clever movement of Nehemiah Moshesh, who under his father's directions hastened across the Drakensberg with a few followers, and located himself on the headwaters of the Umzimvubu before the others could be got away. Nehemiah's presence there prevented the settlement of his father's opponents, who would have established a rival Basuto power in Nomansland, as the country below the Drakensberg had now come to be termed. It led also to the claim which in later times the Basuto chiefs set up to the present district of Matatiele as part of their country. At first the most persevering efforts were made by Nehemiah to obtain Sir George Grey's recognition of his right to the land there, and when these failed, the old chief Moshesh advanced a claim on the ground of a cession of the district to him by Faku. But the claim has never been recognised by any British or Colonial authority, and a Commission which investigated it in 1875 came to a decision adverse to the Basuto pretensions.

Sir George Grey also proposed to remove the Griqua chief Adam Kok from the district of Philippolis in the Free State to a part of Nomansland. The Griquas were a mixed body of people, chiefly of Hottentot blood, who had been residing about the junction of the Vaal and Orange rivers since the beginning of the century. Adam Kok was in alliance with the British Government. His followers were believed to be making rapid progress in civilization, and as they had sold most of their ground to European farmers, Sir George Grey thought of locating them as British subjects in a new and more fertile country, where they would have room to expand.

Early in 1861 the Governor determined to pay a visit in person to the country between the Umtata and Umzimkulu, to make arrangements for the location of the Griquas in the uplands, and to ascertain for himself the cause of the constant commotions in the inhabited parts, so that he might be able to devise a remedy. But he fell ill at King William's Town, and was therefore obliged to send some trusty person in his stead. Sir Walter Currie, Commandant of the Frontier Armed and Mounted Police, was the one upon whom his choice fell. That gentleman proceeded upon the mission, and as a preliminary step paid a visit to Faku. The Rev. Thomas Jenkins, a Wesleyan missionary who possessed the confidence of the Pondo chief, was present at the interview, as were also the great councillors of the tribe. Faku asserted his personal desire for peace, and accused his enemies of being the cause of the disturbances. He thought the Colonial Government would be able to keep them in better order than he could, and he therefore offered to cede the whole country between the Drakensberg and a line which he named, extending from the Umtata to the Umzimkulu, upon condition of the Government exercising direct rule over it. The line named by Faku is that which divides Pondoland from the present Chief Magistracy of Griqualand East, then generally called Nomansland.

It was a very politic offer, this of the clever Pondo chief. He had been for years vainly endeavouring to reduce his enemies to subjection, and now he proposed to hand most of them over to the Colonial Government to be kept quiet, while he crushed or absorbed the rest. That is not the light in which the cession was regarded by the Government, but there can be no doubt of it being Faku's secret view. The line left him more land than he ever actually had under his control before, and it left his enemies within it entirely at his mercy. That the offer thus made in March 1861, though considered by the Government thenceforth as binding upon the Pondos, was not fully acted upon for years afterwards, was no fault of Faku.

Sir Walter Currie went carefully over the proposed line, and visited the chiefs living beyond it. He found each of them professing a desire for peace and endeavouring to throw the blame of the disturbances upon some of the others. All expressed a wish to be taken under the protection of the Government, and a willingness to receive magistrates.

In 1862 Sir Philip Wodehouse located the Griquas in that part of Nomansland east of the Umzimvubu which is now comprised in the districts of Kokstad and Umzimkulu. It is from them that the whole territory has since received its present name. The object of placing them there was to establish in Nomansland a power, acting under British prestige, believed to be sufficiently civilized to set a good example and sufficiently powerful to maintain order. But the scheme was an utter failure, and in a few years Adam Kok was obliged to ask that a British Resident should be stationed in the country to endeavour to keep the different sections of the inhabitants from exterminating each other.

Kok was able to perform one service, however, in driving Nehemiah Moshesh out of the country. That individual had been doing his utmost to extend Basuto influence. When the Griquas left the Free State they moved into Basutoland, where they remained for about two years before they crossed the Drakensberg. Old Moshesh was desirous that Kok should settle in Nomansland as his vassal, and as the Griqua Captain did not do so, Nehemiah was strengthened for the purpose of annoying him. The Basutos managed to plunder the Griquas of a good many cattle, but ultimately Nehemiah and his robber band were attacked and compelled to recross the Drakensberg.

The wars which began in 1865 between the Basutos and the Free State drove a considerable number of people into Nomansland. In 1867 the Monaheng clan under Lebenya abandoned Basutoland and crossed over the mountains into the waste country below. Another large clan followed under Makwai, the chief of highest rank in the house of Moshesh, when his stronghold was captured by the Free State forces. These served as centres of attraction, to which different small parties were subsequently drawn.   There went over also from the Wittebergen Native Reserve (now Herschel) the Batlokoa clan under the chief Lehana, son of the celebrated Sikonyela, the lifelong enemy of Moshesh. In March 1869, just after the Convention of Aliwal North was arranged, Sir Philip Wodehouse crossed over into Nomansland, taking with him from Herschel the Hlubi chief Zibi, grandson of Mpangazita, with his clan.   Another section of the Hlubi tribe, under the chief Ludidi, a younger brother of Langalibalele, had been resident in the country for some years.   To all the recent immigrants the Governor gave locations along the base of the Drakensberg.   Makwai, he placed under Adam Kok, and extended the Griqua district westward to the Kenigha river, thus including in it the whole of Matatiele.   Lebenya and Zibi he placed together, giving them the ground from the Kenigha to the Tina, without laying down any boundary between them.   The land between the Tina and the Eland's river he gave to Lehana.

In January 1872 a Commission, consisting of Messrs. C. D. Griffiths, Governor's Agent in Basutoland, James Ayliff, Resident Magistrate of Wodehouse, and J. Murray Grant, Inspector of the Frontier Armed and Mounted Police, was appointed to investigate the cause of the dissensions in Nomansland and to arrange boundaries between the various tribes and clans.

The Commission found the country in a state of almost indescribable confusion.   Everywhere traces of burnt villages and devasted gardens were to be seen, while there was hardly a clan that did not regard its neighbours as its enemies.   Most of them, however, seemed weary of war and willing to submit to a controlling power.   These asked that the Government should assume direct authority over them all, by sending magistrates into the country, in which case they promised to pay hut tax.   The chiefs who made this request were Makaula, of the Bacas, Umhlonhlo, of the Pondomisis, Lehana, of the Batlokoas, Lebenya, of the Basutos, Ludidi and Zibi, of the Hlubis, and Jojo of the Xesibes.   The last named was living on the Pondo side of the line, all the others were within Nomansland.   Umditshwa held aloof from the Commission.

Umqikela, who had succeeded Faku as paramount chief of the Pondos, objected to interference in the country west of the Umzimvubu, as he denied that any land on this side had been ceded by his father. The Commission, however, recommended to the Government that the line as described by Faku to Sir Walter Currie should be maintained, and the Government decided to adhere to it, as it had been recognised ever since 1861.

Some boundaries were laid down and some promises to keep the peace obtained, but the Commission could do little beyond reporting upon the condition of affairs.   The conclusion it arrived at was embodied in a recommendation that Nomansland should be brought under British authority, and that magistrates should be appointed to exercise jurisdiction over the people.

More than a year went by after the Commission concluded its labours before the Government took any further action. The war between the Gcalekas and Tembus, which occurred at this time, seemed to indicate the necessity of extending Colonial influence and control in the rear of those tribes, and was the immediate cause of the appointment of the first European official in Nomansland.

In July 1873 Mr. Joseph M. Orpen, previously a member of the House of Assembly and an earnest advocate of the extension of British rule over the border tribes, was selected to fill the post of magistrate with a little party of colonial blacks who had settled at the Gatberg, and with the clans of Lehana, Lebenya, and Zibi. He was also appointed British Resident for the whole of Nomansland.

Upon his arrival, Mr. Orpen found that war was being carried on by the Pondo chief Ndamase against Umhlonhlo, and that the rival sections of the Pondomisi were as usual fighting with each other. The Pondos were gaining an ascendency over their divided opponents, and there seemed a likelihood that they would be able to crush them all at no very distant date. Mr. Orpen immediately organised the Fingo, Batlokoa, and Basuto clans under him as a military force, and called upon Adam Kok for assistance. In September he visited Umhlonhlo and Umditshwa, who both again made overtures to be received under British protection and promised to lay down their arms. Then, feeling confident that the Pondos would hesitate before coming into collision with the Government, he called upon them to cease hostilities. They did so, and within a few weeks there was peace throughout the territory.

In October the Secretary for Native Affairs authorized Mr. Orpen to announce to Umhlonhlo and Umditshwa that they and their people were received as British subjects. Makaula and Makwai had repeated their applications, but the Government considered it advisable to let their cases stand over for a while, as they were not pressing. Formal notification of their acceptance was made to the two Pondomisi chiefs on the 22nd of October, and information thereof was sent to Umqikela and Ndamase. These chiefs objected, first to the line from the Umtata to the Umzimvubu between Nomansland and Pondoland, secondly to the reception as British subjects of chiefs and people whom they claimed as being under their jurisdiction, and thirdly to the appointment of British officials in Pondo territory without their consent. But they declared that they had every desire to remain at peace with the Colonial Government, and would therefore respect the new arrangement.

The failure of Langalibalele's rebellion in Natal did much to strengthen the authority of Government in Nomansland. On the 4th of November 1873 three Europeans and two natives were shot down by the rebels in the Bushman's Pass. The Hlubis were at the time removing their cattle from Natal, and it was believed that they intended to retire to Nomansland where they had many relatives living under Ludidi, Langalibalele's brother, Zibi, Langalibalele's second cousin, and several other petty chiefs. It was known that there was a good understanding between the rebels and a great many other clans. The danger of a general rising was therefore imminent.

The Cape Government with all haste sent detachments of the Frontier Armed and Mounted Police to Basutoland and Nomansland; the Natal Government despatched the volunteers of that Colony with native auxiliaries in pursuit of the rebels; and Mr. Orpen, though less than four months in Nomansland, raised a force of Batlokoas, Basutos, and Griquas, to prevent Langalibalele from entering that territory. As soon as it was ascertained that the Hlubis were retiring into Basutoland, Inspector Grant with two hundred of the police left Nomansland to cross the mountains, and with him went Mr. Orpen and two hundred and thirty-five picked men under Lehana and Lebenya· But the country they had to traverse was the most rugged in South Africa, so that they did not reach Basutoland until after the surrender of Langalibalele.

The dispersion of the Hlubis, the confiscation of their cattle, and the banishment of their chief followed. To all the tribes, but particularly to those in Nomansland where the conflicting elements were more numerous than elsewhere, the fate of the rebels was a lesson that the Government was strong enough to enforce order. The clans, though weary of their perpetual feuds, would certainly not have submitted to our rule for any cause except that of respect for power. We flatter ourselves by speaking of our greater wisdom, clemency, sense of justice, etc., but no untutored native respects us for any other quality than our superior strength.

After the reception of Umhlonhlo and Umditshwa as British subjects in 1873, Mr. Orpen took up his residence at Tsolo in the Pondomisi district, his object being to establish the authority of the Government there in something more than name. He found the chiefs Umhlonhlo and Umditshwa altogether opposed to any interference with their people. Though the system of government by means of magistrates had been thoroughly explained to them and they had applied to be accepted as British subjects with full knowledge of what the effect upon themselves would be, they now remonstrated against any deprivation of their former power. Each of them was putting people to death on charges of witchcraft, or merely from caprice. Umhlonhlo refused even to allow a census of his people to be taken.

In this case, as in so many others, the dissensions among the clans presented a lever to work with. Mr. Orpen explained how easily he could bring about a combination of opponents to crush any one who should resist him, and how slow friends would be in coming to assist against a power that had just punished Langalibalele so severely. The two chiefs understood the situation, and without much ado made a show of submission. They were both charged with murder, tried in open court, found guilty, and fined.

The next event of importance in the territory was the establishment of colonial authority in Adam Kok's district. The Griquas had moved there as British subjects, but they had never received protection or in any way been interfered with. Adam Kok was getting old, and was without an heir. In 1874 he had nominally some thirty-six thousand subjects, but only four thousand one hundred were Griquas, the remainder being aliens, Fingos, Basutos, Bacas, and others who had settled on ground given to him by the Government. The demands made upon him by Mr. Orpen for assistance, first against the Pondos, and next against Langalibalele, showed him the anomalous position in which he was placed. He asked that he should either be recognised as an independent chief, or be granted the rights and privileges of a British subject.

On the 16th of October 1874, Governor Sir Henry Barkly, who was then making a tour through the native territories, met the Griqua chief and the members of his Council at Kokstad. Mr. Orpen, the British Resident in Nomansland, was with the Governor. The question of Adam Kok's position was discussed, and a provisional agreement was made for the assumption of direct authority over the country by the Colonial Government. The official books and documents were handed over to Mr. Orpen by the Griqua Secretary, and the territory was added by the Governor to that already under his charge, with the understanding that all existing institutions were to remain undisturbed for the time being.

In February 1875 Messrs. Donald Strachan, a magistrate under Adam Kok, and G. C. Brisley, Secretary of the Griqua Government, arrived in Cape Town as representatives of the Griqua chief and people, and concluded the arrangements. Kok was to retain his title of Chief, be paid a salary of £700 per annum, and have joint authority with a Commissioner who should correspond directly with the Secretary for Native Affairs. The members of the Griqua Council were to receive small annuities and all undisputed titles to land issued by the Griqua Government were to be confirmed. With these conditions all except a few lawless individuals were satisfied. Mr. Thomas A. Cumming, Superintendent of Idutywa, was appointed Acting Commissioner, and assumed duty at Kokstad on the 25th of March 1875. Practically he carried on the government, as Kok left nearly everything in his hands. A petition against the change thus brought about was prepared by the disaffected party, but it only proved their weakness, for when forwarded to Cape Town it contained no more than one hundred and thirty-one signatures. Captain Kok wrote to the Government, protesting against its being considered as of any importance, and stating that three-fourths of the signatures were those of persons who had neither position nor property in the country.

The territory thus added to our rule is that comprised in the three districts of Umzimkulu, Kokstad, and Matatiele. These districts were indeed formed under the Griqua Government, and the same divisions continued to be recognized by the colonial authorities. Mr. Donald

Strachan remained magistrate of Umzimkulu, and Mr. Cumming performed the same duties at Kokstad. Matatiele was left for a time without a magistrate. In these districts there were besides the Griquas, the Basutos under Makwai, the Hlubis under Ludidi, the Hlangwenis under Sidoyi, and a great many other Bantu clans, all of whom gladly became British subjects.

On the 30th of December 1875 Adam Kok died. The nominal dual authority then ceased, as he had no successor. A few months later Captain Blyth was appointed Chief Magistrate of the three Griqua districts, and assumed duty in March 1876, Mr. Cumming returning to Idutywa. On his arrival at Kokstad Captain Blyth found a rebellious spirit still existing among some of the Griquas, but as he was accompanied by a strong police force he had no difficulty in suppressing it. He placed two of the disaffected residents under arrest, and disarmed the others, after which there was no open display of sedition.

He soon found that much more serious danger was to be apprehended from the designs of Nehemiah Moshesh. That individual in 1875 had the assurance to bring his pretensions to the ownership of Matatiele by petition before the Colonial Parliament, and one of the objects of a Commission appointed in July of that year was to investigate his claim. The Commission consisted of Messrs. C. D. Griffith, Governor's Agent in Basutoland, S. A. Probart, Member of the Legislative Assembly, and T. A. Cumming, Acting Commissioner with Adam Kok. After a long and patient examination, these gentlemen decided that Nehemiah had forfeited any right he might ever have had through promises of Sir George Grey and Sir Philip Wodehouse to allow him to remain in Matatiele on good behaviour. Even before this decision was known he had been holding political meetings in the country, Mr. Orpen having permitted him again to take his residence in it; and now he was endeavouring to bring about the union of the native tribes around him, with the evident object of throwing off European control. There could be no such thing as contentment in the land while such a conspirator was at liberty, and Captain Blyth therefore had him arrested. He was subsequently tried in King William's Town and acquitted, but his detention in the meantime enabled the authorities to carry out the law and maintain order.

To the territory under Captain Blyth's administration was added in March 1876 the block of land between Matatiele, the Pondomisi country, and the Pondo boundary line, since called the District of Mount Frere, by the acceptance of the Bacas under Makaula as British subjects. This chief and his councillors had repeatedly requested to be taken over, and their petition had been favourably reported on by the Commission of 1875. The terms under which they became subjects were the usual ones; that in all civil and petty criminal complaints suitors might bring their cases before the magistrate or the chief at their option, that there should be an appeal from the chief to the magistrate, that important criminal cases were to be tried by the magistrate, that no charge of dealing in witchcraft was to be entertained, that on every hut a yearly tax of ten shillings was to be paid, and that the chief was to receive a salary of £100 a year and his councillors certain smaller annuities. Captain Blyth placed Sub-Inspector John Maclean, of the Frontier Armed and Mounted Police, in charge of Makaula's people until the arrival in May 1876 of the magistrate selected by Government, Mr. J. H. Garner, son of a missionary who had long lived with them.

No clan in the whole of the native territories has given greater satisfaction than the people of Mount Frere. The reports have been uniform as to their good conduct, and on several occasions they have shown by their readiness to take the field with our forces that they appreciate the advantages of their present position.

Early in 1878, while the Colony was involved in war with the frontier clans, the disaffected Griquas took up arms under Smith Pommer, a Hottentot from Kat River, and Adam Muis, who had at one time been an official under Adam Kok. They were confident of receiving assistance from the Pondos under Umqikela, and there can be little doubt that if they had been successful at first the whole Pondo army would have joined them. One of the leaders visited Umqikela and returned to the rebel camp with ninety Pondos under command of Josiah Jenkins, an educated nephew of the chief. It was not until Josiah saw that adherence to the insurgent cause meant certain destruction that he and the Pondos under him surrendered to Captain Blyth, when an apology was made for them that they had been sent by Umqikela to deliver up Adam Muis to the Government, but that owing to Josiah's youth and inexperience he had blundered in the manner of carrying out his instructions.

There was at the time a troop of the Cape Mounted Riflemen at Kokstad, which was joined by a few European volunteers, some natives under the refugee chief Sidoyi, and by Makaula's Bacas, who rendered important assistance. In two engagements, on the 14th and 17th of April, the insurgents were defeated, with a loss of thirty-five killed, including Muis and Pommer. Nearly two hundred were made prisoners, and the rebellion was completely stamped out. The districts of Umzimkulu, Kokstad, Matatiele and Mount Frere remained under Captain Blyth's jurisdiction as Chief Magistrate until September 1878, when he was removed to the Transkei. Mr. Strachan continued to be magistrate of Umzimkulu, and Mr. Garner of Mount Frere. Mr. G. P. Stafford was stationed by Captain Blyth at Matatiele, and performed the duty of magistrate until August 1876, when Mr. M. W. Liefeldt was placed there. At Kokstad the Chief Magistrate resided. This arrangement was a continuation of the old order of things, and was in accordance with the recommendation of the Commission of 1875, which had been appointed to enquire into the affairs of the territory. When Captain Blyth left, Mr. C. P. Watermeyer was appointed Acting Chief Magistrate, and held office until the 25th of December following.

We turn now to the country between the Kenigha and Tembuland, which at this time had a population of about twenty-two thousand souls. In April 1875 Mr. Orpen, feeling aggrieved by the stipulation with Messrs. Strachan and Brisley which removed the Griqua districts from his control, resigned his appointment as British Resident in Nomansland, and left the territory. His former clerk, Mr. Fred P. Gladwin, was then instructed to act until arrangements could be made for placing magistrates with the different chiefs who had been received as British subjects.

Already one such magistrate had been appointed, to the Gatberg, now known as the District of Maclear, but he had accidently lost his life. Mr. J. R. Thompson was then selected, and assumed duty in November 1875, when the people of Lehana, Lebenya, and Zibi were first called upon to pay hut tax. These clans were then giving little or no trouble. In 1878 Lebenya and Zibi gave considerable assistance against the rebel Baphutis under Morosi, and the Batlokoas of Lehana were hardly less active, though on that occasion the chief himself was not so zealous as he might have been. We shall have occasion to refer to these clans again in the account of the rebellion in 1880.

The next appointment was that of Mr. M. B. Shaw to the magistracy of the country occupied by Umhlonhlo's people, or the present district of Qumbu. Mr. Shaw assumed duty there in June 1876, and remained until July 1878, when he was succeeded by Mr. Hamilton Hope.

Mr. Gladwin had then only Umditshwa's people in the district of Tsolo to act with. In September 1877 Mr. A. R. Welsh was appointed magistrate with that chief, who had hitherto been giving considerable trouble. He was exceedingly jealous of any interference with his people, but was submissive enough in the presence of a force able to chastise him. This was shown in an almost ludicrous manner on one occasion, when a strong body of police happened to be near by in Tembuland. In 1878 he furnished a contingent of eight hundred men to assist against Stokwe Tyali, but this was when Stokwe's cause was seen to be hopeless.

These three districts, Maclear, Qumbu, and Tsolo, were not subject to the authority of the Chief Magistrates of Griqualand East until the close of 1878, when the consolidation of the different native territories took place. Prior to that date each of the magistrates corresponded directly with the Secretary for Native Affairs, and received instructions from him. But upon the appointment of the Hon. Charles Brownlee, who assumed duty as Chief Magistrate on the 25th of December 1878, the seven districts were united, and the title of Nomansland was lost by the extension of that of Griqualand East to the whole territory.

Henceforth the district of Kokstad was provided with a sub-magistrate so as to leave the head of the territory free to attend to more important matters than those of adjudicating in petty cases. Mr. Geo. W. Hawthorn was appointed, and assumed duty on the 1st of January 1879.

Up to this period the Government had been acting in Griqualand East without any other authority from Parliament than the allowance of the excess of expenses incurred over revenue received. As early as 1861 the Legislative Council, by the casting vote of the President, adopted a Report brought up by a Select Committee, declaring the advisability of British authority being extended over the whole country between the Cape Colony and Natal.   But the discussion on the subject showed that while the Council was equally divided as to interfering with the natives or letting them alone, those who favoured the extension of authority over them differed as to whether they should be ruled by the Imperial or Colonial Government.

In 1873 the Hon. C. Brownlee, then Secretary for Native Affairs, in a Report upon his arrangement of terms of peace between Kreli and Gangelizwe, suggested the extension of colonial authority over the country ceded by Faku.   This Report was submitted to Parliament, and a Committee of the House of Assembly was appointed to consider it, but did not conclude its labours before Parliament was prorogued.

In 1875 the subject was brought by the Ministry before Parliament, and a resolution was adopted by both Houses, declaring that it was "expedient that the country situated between the Umtata and Umzimkulu, commonly known as Nomansland, should be annexed to this Colony, and that the Government take such preliminary steps as may place it in a position to effect such annexation."   On the 30th of June in this year the Governor in his prorogation speech announced that Her Majesty's concurrence in the annexation of Nomansland had already been officially notified to him.

In June 1876 Letters Patent were issued at Westminster, empowering the Governor to proclaim the territory annexed to the Cape Colony, after the legislature should pass a law to that effect.   In 1877 an Annexation Act was passed by the Cape Parliament, and on the 17th of September 1879 the measure was completed by the issue of the Governor's proclamation, to have force from the 1st of the following October.

The country thus became part of the Cape Colony, but as its inhabitants were not sufficiently advanced in civilization to be admitted to the full privileges or to perform the whole duties of burghers, it was made subject to special legislation by the Governor with the advice of the Executive Council.   The proclamation of September 1879 provided that all the laws then in force in the Cape Colony should become the laws of Griqualand East, except in so far as they should be modified by certain regulations published at the same time.   The territory is not represented in the Colonial Parliament, nor are Acts of Parliament enacted since September 1879 in force there unless they are expressly extended to it in the Acts themselves or by proclamation of the Governor in Council.

The year 1880 witnessed the most formidable attempt ever made by natives in South Africa to throw off European supremacy.   The tribes that had come under our control at their own urgent and often repeated request when threatened with destruction by their enemies, as soon as the peril was over demurred to any restraint such as the laws of a civilized Government necessarily imposed upon them.   We had lulled ourselves into the delusion that these people had a high regard for English justice and English benevolence, when it was only English power that they had any respect for.

In April 1880 the Chief Magistrate of Griqualand East began to observe that matters were becoming very unsatisfactory. Outwardly all was as calm as ever. Chiefs and people alike were loud in expressions of loyalty and declarations of satisfaction. But Mr. Brownlee was too experienced in native ways to trust to indications of this kind, and when he ascertained that Basuto messengers were stealthily passing to and fro and that the chiefs were in close correspondence with each other, he knew that a storm was gathering.

There was a small force of Cape Mounted Riflemen in the territory, but early in September it was removed to Basutoland. After this the reports received by Mr. Brownlee became more alarming, and he determined to visit Matatiele, where the greatest danger of disturbance was to be apprehended. On the 11th of September he held a meeting with the Basutos of that magistracy, and received their repeated assurances that no matter what their tribe beyond the mountains might do they would ever be found loyal to the Government.

The Chief Magistrate returned to Kokstad, and there received intelligence of the engagement of the 13th September between Lerothodi and the Cape Mounted Rifles at Mafeteng. Taking with him Mr. Donald Strachan and Mr. George Hawthorn, that gentleman's successor as magistrate of Umzimkulu, with an escort of twenty-five men of the Abalondolozi, Mr. Brownlee left again for Matatiele. He reached the residency on the 30th September, and found the Basutos, who less than three weeks before had been talking so loyally, now arming and singing war songs in all the locations. He endeavoured to pacify them, but in vain. Mr. Liefeldt, the magistrate, enrolled a hundred natives, Hlubis and Basutos whom he believed to be trustworthy, for the defence of the residency, but it was soon ascertained that most of these last were traitors at heart. Forty of them deserted during the night of the 2nd October, and joined the rebels.

On the night of the 3rd of October it was resolved to abandon the residency, as it was not possible to hold it, and to remain longer would expose the little party to certain death. Next morning Messrs. Brownlee, Strachan, Hawthorn, and Liefeldt effected their escape, and a little later in the day the place was surrounded by insurgents, through whom the Hlubis were compelled to cut their way with a loss of eleven men. By this time the whole district of Matatiele was in revolt, the trading stations were being plundered and the mission stations destroyed. The Europeans, after being despoiled of everything, were permitted to retire to Kokstad.

As soon as intelligence of the Basuto insurrection reached Maclear, the magistrate, Mr. J. R. Thompson, enrolled the Fingos and a few colonial blacks who in 1872 had been located in that district, and made the best preparations which he could for the defence of his post. His position was one of great peril, for it was anticipated that the rebels of Matatiele would be joined by their kinsmen in his district.

It was then that Hamilton Hope, magistrate of Qumbu, resolved to aid in the defence of Maclear and at the same time secure the Pondomisis under Umhlonhlo on the side of Government, or perish in the attempt. He had always been on friendly terms with Umhlonhlo, and had treated him with extreme consideration. The chief professed to be attached to the magistrate, and asserted his readiness to act in any way Mr. Hope might direct. To outward appearance there was no reason to suspect him of treacherous intentions. But Mr. Hope knew the character of the people he had to deal with, and he had received abundant warning of the danger he was about to incur. At that time he could easily have escaped to Umtata. But like a brave man and a faithful servant of the Government, as he was, he determined to risk his life in the effort to get Umhlonhlo to commit himself against the rebels, and thus confine the insurrection within narrow bounds.

He arranged with Umhlonhlo to meet him with five hundred men at a camp on the road to Maclear, to which place he would bring all the men he could collect about the residency and such arms and ammunition as could be obtained. His clerk, Mr. Davis, and two young officers on the establishment of the Chief Magistrate of Tembuland, by name Henman and Warrene, accompanied him. Mr. Hope suggested to these gentlemen that they had better not go, as it was sufficient for him alone to incur the risk, but they preferred proceeding to remaining behind and thereby betraying to Umhlonhlo and his people that they were not implicitly trusted.

On the 23rd of October all was ready for the advance. There had been as yet no show of enmity on one side or want of confidence on the other. Umhlonhlo's men ranged themselves in a semicircle for a war dance preparatory to marching, and the Europeans stood by the waggons as observers. As the dance went on, little groups of warriors rushed out from the main body, flourishing their assegais and pretending to stab opponents. Of a sudden one of these groups dashed forward and struck down Messrs. Hope, Henman, and Warrene. Mr. Davis was spared, owing to his being the son of an old missionary with the Pondomisis and the brother of a missionary then with the tribe, the savage chief exclaiming that it was Government only he desired to kill. Three or four hundred snider rifles and twenty-seven thousand rounds of ammunition fell into Umhlonhlo's hands by this act of treachery, which was a signal for a rising of the clans on both sides of the Umtata. The magistrate's horse and gun were given to Roqa and Umbeni, two Pondo messengers who were present at the massacre, and they were directed by Umhlonhlo to take them as a present to Ndabankulu, a brother of the Pondo chief Umqikela, with an intimation of what had been done.

Immediately after the massacre Umhlonhlo joined the rebel Basutos. Mr. Thomson, with forty European volunteers from Dordrecht and one hundred and twenty Batlokoas under Lehana, had in the meantime left Maclear, and was advancing to meet Mr. Hope, when news of the massacre reached him. He had only time to throw his men into a trading station, when he was surrounded by the enemy. Here, though attacked repeatedly, he managed to beat his assailants off and hold the post until the arrival of a column of friendly Natives from Umzimkulu, under Mr. Hawthorn. Mr. Thomson then made a stand at the Maclear residency, where for a month he was cut off from all communication by a host of Basuto, Pondomisi and Tembu rebels, but when reduced to the last extremity for food and ammunition he was rescued by a party of volunteers from Dordrecht.

The massacre by Umhlonhlo took place close to a station in charge of the Rev. Stephen Adonis, a Native missionary. Fearing that he also might be put to death, he sprang upon a horse with only a reim in the mouth, and made all haste to Tsolo. Having informed Mr. Welsh, the magistrate there, of what had occurred, he sped on to Umtata, which post he reached that same night, and gave warning to Major Elliot, chief magistrate of Tembuland.

There was only one building at Tsolo capable of being defended and that was the prison. Its walls were of stone, and it was covered with iron, but it was very small. Mr. Welsh hastily loop-holed it, and then the Europeans, men, women and children, and the Native police took shelter within it. They were not a moment too soon, for Umditshwa's people had already risen, and were even then plundering and burning the trading stations in the district. Next morning at dawn two traders, who had escaped with only their lives, joined them, and then there were shut up in that little building thirty Europeans, of whom eleven only were men, and five Native policemen. They had no more than two hundred rounds of ammunition and a very scanty supply of food. The Pondomisis, mad with war excitement, plundered and destroyed the residency and other buildings before their eyes. Every moment they feared would be their last, though they were resolved to sell their lives dearly. Uditshwa offered, if they would leave the prison, to send them under escort to Umtata, but wretched as they were they could not trust themselves in his hands.

Their only hope was in relief from Umtata. But Major Elliot was himself in almost desperate straits, for many of the clans in the territory under his charge had also risen, his sub-magistracies were abandoned, he was himself in laager, and until Gangelizwe came in he had every reason to believe that all Tembuland was in rebellion. It was eight days before help of any kind could be sent. At last, on Sunday, the 31st October, when they were almost sunk in despair, a column was seen approaching Tsolo. It was a body of Nquiliso's Pondos, led by the Rev. James Morris, and accompanied by six European volunteers from Umtata. Braver men than these seven colonists no country need wish to have. They went with their lives in their hands, for there was no guarantee that Nquiliso's people would not act as Umhlonhlo's had done, and it was certain that at the best these Pondos were not more than lukewarm in rendering assistance. When the relief column reached Tsolo, some of the rescued Europeans, from hunger, anxiety, and the horrible discomforts of such close confinement, were found to be delirious. All, however, were saved, and reached Umtata without further suffering.

Thus the rebellion had spread over the four districts of Matatiele, Maclear, Qumbu, and Tsolo. All the Basutos, except a very few of

Lebenya's followers whose conduct was doubtful, all the Pondomisis, and about three hundred of the Batlokoas, under Ledingwana, nephew of Lehana, were in arms against us. Even some of the Hlubis, to save themselves from destruction, professed to be with the insurgents. On the side of Government there were a score or two of destitute Europeans, as many colonial blacks, and a few hundred Fingos and Batlokoas under Lehana. To the remaining districts, Kokstad, Umzimkulu, and Mount Frere, the rebellion did not not extend, with the exception that one small clan left Kokstad and joined the insurgents.

Intelligence of the simultaneous rising of so many clans, of the massacre by Umhlonhlo, of the murder of several traders, of the pillage and destruction of public buildings, trading establishments, and mission stations, burst upon the Colony like a sudden thunderclap. The difficulties encountered in Basutoland, constantly increasing in magnitude, had previously engrossed public attention. The regular military forces of the Colony had all been sent to meet the bands of Lerothodi and Masupha. The Government therefore called out a large number of burghers, and as fast as they could be raised bodies of volunteers and levies were sent to the front.

Mr. Brownlee on his side speedily had a strong force in the field. There were a good many European farmers who had purchased ground from the Griquas in the districts of Kokstad and Umzimkulu, there were traders scattered over all the districts, and in the village of Kokstad there were a few mechanics. From these sources a small body of volunteers was raised. The Griquas furnished another corps. The Bacas of Nomtsheketshe and Makaula supplied contingents. Sidoyi, chief of the large clan of the Hlangwenis, who had come into Griqualand from Natal many years before, gave great assistance. Another large body that took the field on the side of Government was composed of Natives from Umzimkulu. These people consisted principally of little groups of refugees who had lost their hereditary chiefs, and who had settled in Umzimkulu under Mr. Donald Strachan's protection when he was one of Adam Kok's magistrates. Since that time they had regarded him as their head, and were devoted to him personally. Some time before the rebellion Mr. Strachan had resigned the appointment of magistrate of Umzimkulu, but at Mr. Brownlee's request he now became Commandant-General of Native forces, and was followed to the field by quite a formidable army.

The rebels were then attacked on both sides, and heavy losses were inflicted upon them. The Basutos made a very poor resistance, and soon abandoned Griqualand East altogether and retreated over the mountains. Umhlonhlo's people took their cattle into Eastern Pondoland, where, owing to Umqikela's friendship, they were kept safely, and were restored when the country was again at peace. The clan was dispersed, but efforts made to capture the chief were unsuccessful, and he is at large to this day, though an outlaw. Umditshwa's people took their cattle into Nquiliso's country, but when the rebellion was over the Pondos refused to restore them. They thus lost everything.

On the 14th of January 1881 Umditshwa, with two of his sons of minor rank and six of his councillors, surrendered. They were sent to King William's Town, where in the following September they were put upon their trial before the Circuit Court, when, being found guilty, the chief was sentenced to three years' imprisonment and his sons and councillors to two years hard labour. With the surrender of Umditshwa the rebellion in Griqualand East closed, as the territory was then in full possession of Government forces, and from that date no resistance was offered there.

The Natives who had been in rebellion now began to give themselves up. As fast as they surrendered they were disarmed and temporarily located, pending the decision of the Government as to their final settlement. During the years 1881, 1882 and 1883, they continued to come in from Pondoland and other districts to which they had fled, though to the present day fully one-third of Umditshwa's clan and three of his sons have not surrendered. The rebel Basutos were not permitted to return to Griqualand East.

In June 1883 a commission, consisting of Messrs. C. Brownlee, D. Strachan, and C. P. Watermeyer, was appointed for the purpose of settling the country lately occupied by the rebels. The plan of the Government was that a Reserve of twenty to twenty-five thousand morgen in extent should be laid out for occupation by Europeans around the seats of magistracy of Qumbu and Tsolo, the remainder of those districts being allotted to Natives. All who had not taken part in the rebellion in Maclear and Matatiele were to be invited to remove to Qumbu or Tsolo, but if they should not choose to do so they were to have locations secured to them where they were. The rest of the country was to be laid out in farms and sold to Europeans.

The Commission was engaged for some months in defining locations and settling in them the various applicants for land. A large part of the district of Qumbu was given to Fingos, comprising (a) a clan under Ludidi, who moved from Matatiele, (b) a clan under Umtengwane, son son of Ludidi, who came from Mount Frere, (c) a clan under Nelani, who came also from Mount Frere, (d) surplus population from the Izeli Valley in the Division of King William's Town, and (e) a clan under the headman Maqubo. The Pondomisis had an extensive location assigned to them, in which they were placed under the headman Umzansi, a brother of Umhlonhlo. Another tract of land was set apart for a body of Basutos under Sofonia Moshesh. People of different tribes mixed together were placed in locations under Jonas and Umntonintshe. The Wesleyan Mission station of Shawbury had a large block of land assigned to its dependents. And around the seat of magistracy, some twenty thousand morgen, the remainder of the district, were reserved for the use of Europeans.

The district of Tsolo, with the exception of a Reserve of some twenty-three thousand morgen about the seat of magistracy, was likewise entirely parcelled out among natives. Here also the Fingos received large allotments. A number of these people moved in from the district of Maclear, and to those from the Izeli a section was assigned, bordering on their ground in Qumbu. The late rebel

Pondomisis, over whom Mabasa, uncle of Umditshwa, was placed as headman, received a large location. Ground was assigned to the Tolas under Bikwe, a clan which migrated from Pondoland in 1882. Four other locations, under as many headmen, were given to people of various clans, among whom were a good many Pondomisis. The mission of the Church of England was provided with ground on which to re-establish its destroyed station of St. Augustine. And several deserving natives received farms from five hundred to a thousand acres in extent as quitrent grants.

The old district of Maclear was in 1882 divided into two magisterial districts, named Maclear and Mount Fletcher. The latter was left by the Commission almost entirely in possession of natives. This district contains the old location of the Hlubis under Zibi, intact, the location of the Batlokoas under Lehana, of which a portion is now set apart for occupation by Europeans, and as much of Lebenya's old location as the Commission considered was needed by those of his people who professed to be loyal.

The present district of Maclear contains one large location of Fingos mixed with people of various clans, and several farms occupied by coloured people, but the greater portion of it has been retained for Europeans. A number of quitrent farms were surveyed there and sold by public auction even before the appointment of the Commission.

In the district of Matatiele about one fourth of the land was laid out into locations. These were assigned to Basutos under George Moshesh, Tsita Moshesh, Klein Jonas, Sibi, and Ramhlagwana, some of them recent refugees from Basutoland, others individuals who went into rebellion but subsequently joined our forces when they appeared in strength ; Baphutis under Masakala, who were also rebel and loyal by turns; Fingos under Mahlangala, Umgubo, Lupindo, Bubesi, Matandela, Manguzela, and others; and a section of the Hlangweni clan which migrated from Umzimkulu under Umzongwana, son of the late chief Sidoyi. The remainder of this district has been reserved for occupation by Europeans.

The removal of the Fingos from the District of Mount Frere made room there for the Bacas under Nomtsheketshe to move in from the Rode valley in Pondoland. This did away with one of the elements of confusion on the southern border. The Bacas and Pondos in the Rode were continually quarrelling, and there was such strong sympathy between the former and their kinsmen under Makaula that there was an ever present danger of these being drawn into conflicts which might terminate in a general war. Now all are subject to colonial authority. Nomtsheketshe is by descent of higher rank than Makaula, but his following is much smaller.

The area of the four rebel districts is about five thousand eight hundred square miles. The settlement effected gave 4,200 square miles to natives, and left 1,600 square miles for occupation by Europeans. A portion of this adjoins the Engcobo district in Tembuland, now partly in possession of Europeans who are too few in number to hold their own in the event of another rebellion. This portion is therefore specially valuable, and if occupied by farmers it will convert a weak and exposed community into a strong line of defence. At present in the whole territory of Griqualand East there are from five to six hundred farms held by Europeans, most of which have been purchased from Adam Kok's people.

A considerable military force is maintained in Griqualand East. The headquarters of the Cape Infantry are at Kokstad, and there are detachments at Maclear, Tsolo, Qumbu and Mount Frere. Detachments of the Cape Mounted Rifles are stationed at Matatiele, Mount Fletcher, Tsolo, Qumbu and Mount Frere.

The population of the Chief Magistracy in 1879 was rather over 74,000. In 1881, just after the rebellion, it was about 50,000. It is now probably greater than in 1879.

The Act No. 40 of 1882 gave the Eastern Districts Court concurrent jurisdiction with the Supreme Court over Griqualand East. Persons charged with crimes punishable by death are now sent for trial to the nearest town where a session of the Circuit Court is held. The magistrates have jurisdiction in all other criminal cases, but their sentences are subject to review by the Chief Magistrate. Civil cases to any amount are tried in the Magistrates' Courts, but there is an appeal to either the Chief Magistrate, the Eastern Districts Court, or the Supreme Court, as the suitors may elect. In criminal cases an appeal may be made as provided in Section 4 of the Resident Magistrate's Court Act of 1876.

Kokstad, the only town in the Chief Magistracy, has become a place of considerable commercial importance within the last ten years. It is built on a broad valley on the banks of the Umzimhlava, a tributary of the Umzimvubu. Three miles from the town rises Mount Currie to the height of seven thousand six hundred feet above ocean level, a very grand object on the landscape. Kokstad contains several churches, a first class public school, a branch of the Standard Bank, and a good many well built stores and dwelling houses. The Act No. 27 of 1882, for the suppression and punishment of certain municipal offences, has been extended by proclamation to the town.

There are at present in Griqualand East, beside the military and the police establishments, twenty-three European officials, viz., one Chief Magistrate, eight Sub-Magistrates, one Accountant, eleven clerks, and two District Surgeons.

The Hon. Charles Brownlee, C.M.G., is Chief Magistrate. He assumed duty in December 1878. He is at present absent on leave, and since the 1st of September 1884 Mr. W. B. Chalmers has been acting.

The following list shows the succession of sub-magistrates:—

MACLEAR :	Mr. J. R. Thomson.
	Mr. L. S. Cole, May 1882.
	Mr. M. B. Shaw, November 1884.
MT. FLETCHER :	Mr. W. P. Leary, September 1882.
	Mr. W. H. Read, May 1883.

QUMBU :	Mr. H. Hope.
	Mr. W. T. Brownlee, July 1881.
TSOLO :	Mr. A. R. Welsh.
	Mr. D. Hook, December 1884.
MATATIELE :	Mr. M. W. Liefeldt.
	Mr. E. S. Rolland, July 1883.
KOKSTAD :	Mr. G. W. Hawthorn.
	Mr. J. T. Wylde, May 1880.
UMZIMKULU :	Mr. D. Strachan.
	Mr. G. W. Hawthorn, May 1880.
	Mr. J. T. O'Connor, December 1881.
MOUNT FRERE :	Mr. J. H. Garner.
	Mr. W. B. Blenkins, April 1880.
	Mr. J. S. Simpson, August 1882.
	Mr. E. G. Whindus, July 1883.
	Mr. W. G. Cumming, September 1884.

DISTRICT OF MOUNT AYLIFF.

Attached to the Chief Magistracy of Griqualand East, but not annexed to the Colony, is a tract of land about two hundred and forty square miles in extent, occupied by the Xesibe clan under the chief Jojo. This slip of country, now called the District of Mount Ayliff, lies along the northern border of Pondoland, between the Rode and the headwaters of the Umtamvuna River. It has the District of Kokstad on the North and the County of Alfred in Natal on the East. Its southern boundary was not defined when the clan was taken over, but was understood to be where Xesibe kraals ended and Pondo kraals began. It was attached to the Chief Magistracy of Griqualand East in 1878.

At that time the conduct of the paramount Pondo chief Um-qikela was held by the Colonial Government to be very unfriendly. There were certain stipulations as to the surrender of criminals, the freedom of roads, the prevention of illicit trade, and the reference of disputes with neighbouring tribes to the mediation of the Cape authorities, contained in the 3rd, 7th, 8th, and 10th clauses of the Maitland treaty of 1844, which the chief practically declined to carry out. In consequence of this measures were taken to extend the dominion of the Colony. Messrs. Blyth and Elliot were commissioned to settle the Pondo difficulty, and by them the chiefs of the border clans were invited to transfer their allegiance to the British Government, which several of them were very ready to do.

The first who responded to this invitation was the Xesibe chief Jojo whose clan numbered about four thousand two hundred souls. He had frequently requested British protection against the Pondos, between whom and his people there was a long and bitter feud. The Commission of 1872 had made the Xesibes tributary to the Pondos, upon the conditions that the territory which they occupied should be left to them intact, and that the Pondos should deal with them fairly. They complained that these terms had not been observed, and the Government then interfered, basing its right to do so upon the 13th clause of the Maitland treaty of 1844. Umqikela asserted that Jojo refused to recognise his authority, which compelled him to treat the Xesibes as rebels. Sir Henry Barkly then required Jojo to recognise Umqikela's paramountcy in a formal manner, and in November 1874 Mr. Strachan accompanied the Xesibe messengers to the Pondo chief and was a witness of their payment to him of eight oxen and two horses as a token of their dependence. Umqikela expressed himself satisfied, and promised to treat the Xesibes as his vassals in a just and liberal manner; but the ill feeling between the two tribes was too deeply seated to be so easily eradicated, and Mr. Strachan was hardly home when the plundering and retaliation commenced again. From that time there was no intermission of these disorders, while fresh appeals for British protection were made by the Xesibes on every suitable opportunity. On the 8th of July 1878 Jojo and his people were accepted as subjects on the usual terms by Messrs. Blyth and Elliot.

The next to respond was a Hlubi named William Nota, who occupied part of the Rode valley, a narrow wedge of land on the Pondo side of the line, between the districts occupied by Makaula's Bacas and Jojo's Xesibes. Nota was a recent immigrant, and had been made by Umqikela headman over a party of Hlubis who occupied the Rode conjointly with some Bacas under the chief Nomtsheketshe and some straggling Xesibes. He had no complaints against the Pondos but had a vague desire to become a "Government man" like the rest of the Hlubis. On the 22nd of July 1878 he was accepted as a subject by the Commissioners, but their act was not confirmed by the Government, and Nota was obliged to make his peace again with Umqikela, which did not occasion much difficulty.

Following Nota came Siyoyo, chief of the Amacwera, a clan claiming to be a remote offshoot of the Pondomisi tribe. He was a vassal of the Pondos with, as a matter of course, a feud with his next neighbour, the Pondo clan under Valelo. Siyoyo had applied in 1877 for protection, by which he meant assistance in his quarrel. He now repeated his desire to become a British subject, and on the 5th of August was accepted by the Commissioners. As in Nota's case, however, the Government declined its ratification, and Siyoyo was obliged to renew his allegiance to Umqikela by formal submission and payment of tribute.

Shortly after this the Hon. William Ayliff, then Secretary for Native Affairs, visited the country. On the 28th of October, 1878, he held a meeting with the Xesibes under Jojo, when he announced that the Government had confirmed the act of the Commissioners in receiving them as subjects. Mr. Walter H. Read was at the same time stationed with them as magistrate.

This procedure of the Government has always been a grievance with the Pondos. The feud between the two tribes was deepened by it, and disturbances became even more frequent than before. In 1879 the Pondo chiefs on the border invaded the district and devastated a large portion of it, burning and destroying the villages as they advanced. They were only checked by the arrival of a force of two thousand five hundred men which was hastily raised in the Umzimkulu district, and sent under Mr. D. Strachan to protect the Xesibes. Umqikela then disowned the acts of the border chiefs and promised to make good the damage done, but failed to do so when Mr. Strachan's army was disbanded.

During the rebellion of 1880 the Xesibes were an element of weakness to us, for as soon as the Colonial forces were withdrawn the Pondos endeavoured to worry them into open war. Instead of giving help in the field, they were clamouring for assistance themselves. So onerous has the protection of this clan been that at one time it was in contemplation to remove them altogether and give them land in one of the districts of Griqualand East. This plan of settling the question was, however, frustrated by the refusal of the Xesibes to leave their district.

The encroachments of the Pondos at length compelled the Government to lay down a line between them and the Xesibes, and in April 1883, a commission consisting of Messrs. C. Brownlee, D. Strachan, C. P. Watermeyer and J. Oxley Oxland, was appointed for that purpose. Umqikela was invited to co-operate with the Commission by sending representatives to assist in defining a boundary, but he declined to do so. His view of the question is tersely summed up in a single sentence in a letter written in his name to the Commissioners by his principal adviser and Secretary Umhlangazo:

"The paramount Chief refuses to recognise the right of the Cape Government to make a boundary in Pondoland between himself and rebel subjects, and will rigidly adhere to the boundary as defined by the Commissioner appointed by Sir Henry Barkly in 1872."

The Commission was therefore obliged to lay down a line without any assistance. In doing so, it gave to the Pondos all places of doubtful ownership and even several villages from which Xesibes had recently been expelled but which were then occupied by Pondos.

The Government is obliged to maintain a much larger military force in Mount Ayliff than in any other district in the Native territories. There are detachments of both cavalry and infantry at the seat of Magistracy and also at the post named Fort Donald. Until recently there was a strong force of Native police kept up, but this has been disbanded.

Notwithstanding the heavy burden to the Colony which these Xesibes have been they are dissatisfied at not having received greater protection. They complain that when they steal from the Pondos the Magistrate punishes them and compels them to restore the booty, but that when the Pondos steal from them the Government does not see that they get redress and Umqikela takes no notice of representations made through our officials. They want, in short, that in return for calling themselves British subjects, the Government should either line their border with troops and police, or give them military aid whenever they can make up a plausible case for retaliating on a Pondo kraal.

The Xesibes pay a yearly hut tax of ten shillings. Native law only is administered in their district.

Mr. W. H. Read was succeeded in May, 1883, by Mr. W. P. Leary, the present magistrate.

The revenue collected in the Chief Magistracy of Griqualand East during the four years and a half ending on the 31st of December, 1883, was £57,040 16s. 1d., the civil expenditure during the same period was £113,696 19s. 4d. or £56,656 3s. 3d. in excess of the revenue. The remarks in the papers on the Transkei and Tembuland concerning the the very large proportion of the revenue expended on schools do not apply to Griqualand East. Here only a sum of £9,084 3s. 11d. or 16 per cent. of the revenue, was devoted to educational purposes.

In the year ending 31st of December 1884 the revenue of Griqualand East and Mount Ayliff (exclusive of reimbursement to the amount of £2,939 16s. 5d.) was £22,526 2s. 11d. made up of the following items: Land, (Hut Tax and Quitrent) £13,772 12s. 0d., Stamps £2,100 12s. 9d., Transfer Dues £1,985, Licences £1,829 12s. 6d., Fines, Forfeitures, etc., £1,231 16s. 9d., Land Sales £990. Telegraph receipts £354 12s. 8d., and Miscellaneous Receipts £261 16s. 3d.

The civil expenditure in the chief Magistracy of Griqualand East during the year ending 31st December, 1884, is given by the Audit Office as follows:—

Ordinary Expenditure	...	...			£16,448	5	3
Education	...	...	...	..	2557	7	4
Stationery	...	...	...	...	119	8	0
Survey Expenses	...	...	...		1817	11	3
Telegraphs	...	...	...	...	1233	13	3
Post Offices	...	...	...	...	326	5	10
					£22,502	10	11

Besides this there is a portion not yet adjusted of the sum of £7,820 0s. 8d. expended in public works during 1884 in the three Chief Magistracies of Transkei, Tembuland, and Griqualand East.

GEO. M. THEAL.

PONDOLAND.

(BLUE BOOK ON NATIVE AFFAIRS 1885).

The Pondos are the only people south of Natal who are now in a condition of independence. There is no interference by any external authority in the government of the people by their chiefs, but as the country is enclosed by territory under Colonial rule, their dealings with other tribes are necessarily subject to Colonial control. Pondoland lies between the Umtata and Umtamvuna rivers, and between Griqualand East and the sea. It has an area of about three thousand eight hundred and sixty-nine square miles, and a population of which the lowest estimate made by competent persons is two hundred thousand souls.

The Pondo tribe is one of those mentioned by the wrecked seamen of the "Stavenisse" in 1686. It was then found between the tribes of the Abambo and the Abatembu, in its present position, though the limits of its possessions at that time can not be ascertained. For the next hundred years there appears to have been no intercourse between these people and Europeans, of which a record has been preserved. In 1790-91 an expedition under the leadership of Mr. Jacob van Reenen travelled from the Cape Colony through Kafirland to the mouth of the Umzimkulu in search of survivors from the wreck of the English East Indiaman "Grosvenor," which was lost on the coast of Pondoland on the 4th of August 1782. Several accounts of the wreck were published within the next ten years, from the narratives of seamen who made their way overland to the Colony; and the journal of Mr. van Reenen's expedition followed in 1792. These, however, throw little or no light upon the condition of the Pondos at that time.

Mr. van Reenen's party visited a village in which they found three aged white women, survivors of a wreck which must have taken place on the coast about 1730 or 1740. They had been married to natives, and had a numerous offspring. Depa, the petty Pondo chief with whose people the first mission in the country was established, was a son of one of these women.

From the date of Mr. van Reenen's visit more than thirty years passed by without anything being heard of the Pondo people. About 1825 their name came occasionally to be mentioned in connection with the ravages of Tshaka, and afterwards some particulars concerning them were gathered from the accounts of a few European adventurers at Natal. In July 1828 Major Dundas, Landdrost of Albany, who was on a mission from the Governor of the Cape Colony to the Zulu chief Tshaka, passed through Pondoland and had an interview with the chief Faku, who was then living in the valley of the Umgazi river. The paramount ruler of the Pondos was found dispirited and in a most dejected condition, with only two or three attendants about him. Tshaka's army had swept the country of cattle, and after remaining there a month and a half had left only ten days before Major Dundas's visit. The Pondos had nothing to live upon or to make clothes with. Faku had sent to Hintsa and Vusani for assistance, but had received none, and he was then about to become a vassal of Tshaka.

In May 1829 the Rev. Wm. Shaw visited Faku, at the Umgazi. The country close around was thickly populated, and the people had gathered a plentiful harvest of corn, but had very few cattle. In this year, 1829, Morely mission station was founded by the Rev. Mr. Shepstone among Depa's people. It was destroyed a few months later by the Amakwabi, when the mission family narrowly escaped; but it was subsequently rebuilt in another and better position on the western bank of the Umtata.

In 1830 the Buntingville mission was commenced by the Rev. Messrs. Boyce and Tainton. Faku, who believed the missionaries to be powerful rainmakers, gave them one of the driest sites in the whole country, in the hope of benefiting by the rain which he anticipated they would cause to descend for their own profit. When, however, he found that his expectations were not realized, he granted a much better site elsewhere, and the mission was removed.

From this time there is abundant material in existence for compiling an account of the Pondo people. There are, in addition to the official records, many statements since made by individual Pondos and published, besides printed reports and letters of missionaries, and references by travellers in several books. Among these last the most important are to be found in "Travels and Researches in Caffraria," by the Rev. Stephen Kay, one volume, London, 1833; "Travels and Adventures in Eastern Africa," by Nathaniel Isaacs, two volumes, London, 1836; and "Narratives of a Journey to the Zoolu Country in South Africa," by Captain Allen F. Gardiner, R.N., one volume, London, 1836.

From these sources it can be ascertained that the Pondo tribe suffered very severely by the wars of Tshaka. It was not alone invasions of their country by armies under that dreaded chief's commanders that harrassed them. Numerous hordes, fleeing before the Zulu spear, sought refuge in the rugged district between the Umzimkulu and Umzimvubu rivers, others made a pathway through it to safer regions beyond. Every horde that came was an enemy to all the rest, and so there was for years a continual scene of pillaging and butchering throughout the land.

It would be a waste of time to search out and place on record the titles of all the clans that made their appearance in Pondoland at this period, let alone to trace their history. Those of them who, like the Bacas, have at present a separate position there, have been mentioned in other chapters. Those who, like many clans of the Abambo, are now incorporated with the Pondos, need no special reference. With a single exception those who have since perished utterly may well remain in oblivion.

The massacre of a party of Europeans makes the exception necessary of a horde called the Amakwabi, under a chief named Qeto. They came down from Zululand, and were proceeding toward the Umtata when they were attacked and turned back by the Pondomisi. They then fell upon the Pondos, and committed fearful ravages. In September 1829 they were visited by three English traders, Lieutenant

Farewell and Messrs. Walker and Thackwray, who were proceeding from the Cape Colony to Natal. The Europeans were well received, and a hut was given them to sleep in. But just before daylight next morning the hut was surrounded, and the white men with their attendants were treacherously murdered. Their waggons, oxen, and goods were then appropriated by Qeto. The next exploit of the Amakwabi was the destruction of Morley mission station. But shortly after this event their career came to a sudden close. Faku managed to draw them into an ambush, where they were attacked by overwhelming numbers, and the entire horde, men, women, and children perished, some by the assegai, others by being hurled over precipices.

In these wars and commotions most of the Pondos were driven to the westward of the Umzimvubu, and the country east of that river became occupied by strangers. Faku himself went to reside in the valley of the Umgazi, and for ten or twelve years at least he was deprived of all authority in what is now called eastern Pondoland.

Early in 1836 an embassy was sent by Governor Sir Benjamin D'Urban to the chiefs Kreli, Vadana, and Faku, for the purpose of establishing a general peace between the tribes and arranging for the return of the missionaries to the stations which, owing to the war between the ama-Xosa and the Colony, had been abandoned in the previous year. A military officer, Captain Delaney of the 75th Regiment, was at its head; and it was intended to make an impression upon the native mind, for it consisted in all of one hundred and ten individuals, of whom eighty were soldiers. It was accompanied by the Rev. Mr. Palmer, who had previously resided in Faku's country, and by Mr. Wm. Fynn as interpreter. On the 5th of February Captain Delaney reached Buntingville, where he met Faku with his councillors and about twelve hundred followers, by whom he was received "with every possible demonstration of pleasure and satisfaction." The report of the embassy contains no information of use at the present day, except the following paragraph.—

"Ncapayi (Kapai as spelt) was prevented attending by the high floods of the rivers, but sent three councillors, who heard the word delivered. They acknowledged Ncapayi to be the ally and subject of Faku. Faku promised to keep his word, and as far as regarded himself would remain at peace with Vadana, Kreli and Buku. At his request, my party manoeuvered on horse and foot, and fired a few shots. This tribe is not so much acquainted with firearms as others, and the effect was greater than I expected. Faku, after receiving the presents, gave me an elephant's tusk for the Governor, one for Colonel Smith, and three for myself."

Much more interesting, when read in the light of subsequent events, is the report of Colonel (afterwards Sir Harry) Smith to Sir Benjamin D'Urban upon the results effected by the embassy. While displaying a want of knowledge of the natives that is almost incomprehensible at the present day, this report gives the earliest indication of the policy of a future Governor. It is dated King William's Town, 20th February 1836, and contains the following paragraphs:—

"Faku had been prepared last year to make war upon Hintsa's country on our behalf. This is effectually stopped, and a mutual peace established.

"Faku for these last two years has only waited for an excuse to wage war on Vadana, and had not the embassy thus proceeded he would have done so. A mutual peace is established.

"All the minor chiefs, seeing the Great Nation, as they term the English, treat only with their most powerful neighbours, will all attach themselves to one or other for protection, or they become the common enemy of this confederation and subject themselves to be annihilated. Vadana's and Faku's tribes are surrounded by several petty chiefs, such as Ncapayi and others, almost banditti;—these have taken alarm at the appearance of British troops and their purpose of establishing a general peace, and are all attaching themselves to a powerful neighbour."

In these reports nothing is said of the extent of the Pondo territory, but in a dispatch from Sir Benjamin D'Urban to Lord Glenelg, of the 16th March 1836, Faku is described as "Chief of the Amapondas on the Umtata, Umgazi, and Umcimvooboo."

In 1837 from the plains of the present Free State long lines of white tilted waggons rolled down the Quathlamba, conveying the Emigrant Boers to Natal. The pioneers found the country from the Tugela to the Umzimvubu almost uninhabited, its former occupants having been driven away or having perished by the Zulu spear. At that time no one spoke or thought of such a thing as Pondo dominion beyond the Umzimvubu. Faku's only chance of existence, indeed, was to keep as quiet as possible, to make no pretensions and to perform no act that would bring Dingaan's wrath upon him.

The Boers settled in the upland pastures of Natal, and being desirous of acquiring a title to the country, their leader, Pieter Retief, applied to Dingaan, Tshaka's brother and successor, for a grant of it. He consented to give it to them in return for a small service, and when this was performed, he affixed his mark to a deed of cession drawn up in the English language by the Rev. Mr. Owen, an English missionary, by which deed the Zulu chief transferred to the Emigrant Boers the whole country from the Tugela to the Umzimvubu. This cession was signed in February 1838. However it may have been regarded by the Zulu chief, whose object in granting it was only to lull the Boers to a feeling of security that he might carry out the dreadful massacres which he afterwards caused to be committed, the document was as binding as any treaty ever made in South Africa. It was the foundation upon which the Boers erected the Republic of Natalia, which, after their victories over Dingaan, they extended northward to the Umvolosi and St. Lucia Bay.

Faku was now safe from the Zulus, and as soon as he realized that he was so, he removed from the Umgazi across the Umzimvubu. The Boers at this time were in correspondence with him, and regarded him as a friendly chief. They did not, however, consider him a potentate of any great importance, but rated his military strength below that of

Ncapayi, the regent of the Bacas. He took up his residence on the Umzimhlava, one of the small streams of what is now Eastern Pondoland.

In December 1840 a commando under Andries Pretorius, with a small auxiliary native force under a petty chief named Fodo, attacked the Bacas of Ncapayi, routed them, and took possession of several thousand head of cattle. There is hardly an event in South African history which has been more severely commented upon and more warmly defended than this. It has been asserted in important official dispatches that the attack was made by a band of lawless freebooters whose sole object was plunder. In documents of equal weight it has been maintained that the attack was justifiable, being made for the purpose of recovering stolen stock; and that Faku himself instigated the farmers to make it, with a view of weakening an old enemy. Enquiries and investigations made of late years prove conclusively that the account of the transaction furnished by the Emigrant Volksraad to Sir George Napier was substantially correct. That account is contained in a lengthy document dated at Pietermaritzburg, 7th April 1841, and is signed on behalf of the Volksraad by J. Prinsloo, the President, and J. J. Burger, the Secretary. It enters fully into the charges of cattlelifting by Ncapayi's people, and contains the following references to Faku:—

" As in the year 1838, we had, by an interchange of letters, concluded a sort of amicable understanding with Faku, we were requested by him in the course of last year to allow Captain Fodo to come to assist him against an attack from Ncapayi. * * When on their march the Commandant, Mr. Pretorius, sent to Faku three of our burghers, who then found that just before arrival Ncapayi had again been in hostile collision with Faku. They even saw some of the killed. Faku was then apprized of our expedition and of its object, and at the same time assured of our friendship and requested to come to the Commandant, who was desirous of taking that opportunity of entering into a permanent treaty of peace with him. He on the other hand expressed himself highly gratified with the mission, but declined to come, on the ground of age and ill health, adding that he deemed it unnecessary to make peace with us, as we had always been friends and never enemies. Our messengers further obtained from Faku and his captains a full confirmation of all the information we had previously received, and also that Ncapayi was our sworn enemy, that he had before in the war with Dingaan offered to assist him against us, and had tried to induce Faku to join him in an attack upon us."

After the collision of the Boers with Ncapayi, Faku's joy at his enemy's losses was blended with fear that the same fate might some day overtake him. In his dealings with white people he had by this time come to be guided entirely by the missionaries, and he now sent messengers to Buntingville to request Mr. Jenkins to pay him a visit. On the 1st of January 1841 the Rev. Messrs. Palmer, Jenkins, and Garner assembled at the chief's residence on the Umzimhlava, where they remained until the 5th, and during that time the course to be pursued was decided upon. A letter was sent to the Governor, who was then on the Colonial frontier, begging that Faku might be taken under his protection, and containing as an enclosure the following declaration:—

"I, Faku, King of the Amapondo, being in great fear of the Boers at Port Natal, in consequence of several reports that have reached me, together with a late attack upon the Amabaca tribe in my immediate neighbourhood, also a peremptory summons for me to appear at the Boers' Camp that had been established in my country, am under the necessity of removing from the land of my Fathers east of the Umzimvooboo; but I hereby declare that I have not abandoned the said country, having only left it for the present in consequence of the circumstances above referred to ; and I hereby desire the missionaries now at my kraal to forward this my letter to the Governor of the Colony, to remain with him as my witness that the land from the Umzimvooboo to the Umzimcooloo belongs to me Faku, king of the Amapondo, and the various tribes tributary to me."

To this document are attached the marks of Faku, Damasi, and Bangasili, and the signatures as witnesses of Saml. Palmer, Thos. Jenkins, and Wm. H. Garner, Wesleyan Missionaries. It is dated Iquankani, Umzimhlovo, January 5th, 1841.

The policy of the Imperial Government at that time was to reduce the size of the European settlement, and to parcel out the whole of South Africa beyond the Colonial border among native chiefs, who were to be brought into alliance by a promise of protection in case of British subjects invading the territories thus given to them. The Province of Queen Adelaide had already been restored to the Rarabes, and our flag had been withdrawn from that extensive district which is now comprised in the Divisions of Wodehouse and Aliwal North. Treaties had been made with a number of petty chiefs and headmen on the immediate border, though it was not until somewhat later that similar agreements were concluded with Adam Kok and Moshesh, and claims to vast tracts of open land in what is now the Orange Free State were thereby given to those chiefs.

Upon receipt of Faku's declaration and the communication from the missionaries who accompanied it, Sir George Napier sent a force of two hundred and fifty men of the 27th Regiment, a few Cape Mounted Riflemen, and some Artillerymen with two field pieces to Pondoland to protect the chief. The expedition was under command of Captain Smith of the 27th. It moved to the Umgazi River, where Faku had formerly resided, and there established itself in a camp made of waggons and temporary earthworks.

The Emigrant Government on being informed by Sir George Napier of his object in sending a military force to Pondoland, replied by explaining minutely their action towards Ncapayi. Regarding the troops they said:—

"It is difficult to understand how Faku could have seen reason to request protection against an attack from us. * * * We are, however, very glad that Your Excellency has stationed a detachment of troops at the Umzimvubu, as we trust that the troops will have sufficient influence to protect Faku against Ncapayi, and that they will also assure the latter that their protection is no license to him to enable him now to plunder us more securely."

After the Farmers had taken possession of Natal, several thousand Bantu refugees of different tribes moved in, and the few natives who had survived the Zulu invasions crept out of the forests in which they had concealed themselves. In August 1841 the Emigrant Volksraad resolved to collect the whole of these people together and to locate them in the district between the Umzimvubu and Umtamvuna rivers, so as to effect a complete separation between them and the Europeans. In that district the blacks were to be left pretty much to themselves, but an officer of the Emigrant Government was to be stationed with them to exercise general control, for they were to be regarded as subjects of the Republic. A copy of this resolution with explanatory statements was forwarded to Sir George Napier by the Volksraad, with the expectation that His Excellency would regard it as a proof of the desire of the Emigrants to deal fairly with the natives.

It had just the contrary effect. The Governor's reply was a Proclamation issued on the 2nd of December 1841, in which he declared that the tract of land referred to formed "part of the Territories belonging to Faku, a Chief at peace with Her Majesty," and announced his determination to take military possession of Natal.

For this purpose Captain Smith was instructed to move on from the Umgazi. On the 1st of April 1842 he began his march. Then followed his defeat by the Boers at Congella, the siege of his camp at D'Urban, and the relief on the 26th of June by Colonel Cloete's expedition.

Natal was wrested from the Boers and became British Colony. But with that well meant though mistaken view of native interests which prevailed in the Colonial Office at the time, its limits were greatly circumscribed. The land between the Tugela and the Umvolosi was restored to the Zulus, which enabled them to build up again that formidable power which the Boers had broken down, and which in 1879 cost so much English blood and treasure to overthrow once more. On the south the district between the Umzimkulu and Umzimvubu was abandoned.

The same policy that gave Adam Kok and a few hundred Griquas a country larger than Scotland, that made Moshesh a great territorial chief, now exerted itself towards the aggrandizement of Faku. On the 7th of October 1844 a treaty was prepared and signed by Sir Peregrine Maitland, at Fort Beaufort, and Messrs. Theophilus Shepstone and William Fynn were then sent to Faku with it. The Rev. Thomas Jenkins explained the different clauses of the document, which Faku unhesitatingly agreed to, and on the 23rd of November the marks of the chief and his son Ndamasi were affixed to it in presence of Messrs. Shepstone, Fynn, and Jenkins, and four of the leading Pondo councillors,

In this treaty Faku is acknowledged as paramount chief over the whole country between the Umtata and Umzimkulu Rivers, from the Quathlamba mountains to the sea, and this territory is secured to him against all claims and pretensions on the part of British subjects. On the other hand it binds him to be the faithful friend of the Colony, to prevent his people from harassing or annoying British subjects passing through his country, to use his best exertions to seize and deliver up refugee criminals, to facilitate the production of evidence, to make restitution for stolen cattle traced to his country, to protect travellers and the post passing through and traders and missionaries residing in his country, to prevent the landing of goods from ships not provided with Colonial licences, to avoid as far as possible making war with neighbouring tribes, to submit to the mediation of the Colonial Government any disputes with other chiefs which he could not settle peaceably, and to aid the Colony with all his forces whenever called upon to do so.

Sir Peregrine Maitland's despatches at this time prove him to have been deplorably ignorant of native politics, but when the treaty was signed he was aware that there were other tribes within the boundaries assigned to Faku, that they were frequently fighting with the Pondos, and that Faku exercised no jurisdiction over them. Of their past history and their claims to independence he knew nothing. But for their protection the treaty contained a provision that "the rights of all petty chiefs and native tribes who have at any period heretofore resided upon any part of the said territory remain unaltered, and they will be at liberty to reside within the said territory in the same manner as they did before they were disturbed by the wars with the Zulu nation."

The objects of this particular treaty have often been misrepresented. It was one of a series which gave to native chiefs claims to vast tracts of land which were not then, and never had been, in their possession. As such, it could not fail to give offence to all except the one favoured tribe. But speculation as to motives is set at rest upon reading Sir Peregrine Maitland's despatch to the Secretary of State, written immediately after the treaty was concluded. He says:—

"My immediate object was to restrain them (the Frontier Kaffirs) from rashly attempting any hostile operations against the Colony, by the knowledge that in case of their doing so they would have in their rear an enemy more powerful than themselves, in alliance with the British Government, and ready to fall upon them with an overwhelming force. But I had other objects in view, and principally three: to secure a friendly neighbour on the south-west boundary of Natal, whereby marauding incursions similar to those by which this Colony has been harrassed may be prevented, to keep open an uninterrupted land communication with Natal through the territory of friendly tribes, and to hinder ships from discharging cargo along the coast between Natal and the Colony, without a licence, to the injury of the revenue."

The condition of the Pondo tribe was by this time very greatly improved. Mrs. Jenkins, the wife of the missionary, who first became acquainted with them in 1838, wrote that they were then in a state of great poverty. They had no cattle of whose skins to make clothing, so the men went entirely naked, and the women wore nothing but a girdle made of maize leaves fastened together and tied round their waists. The different clans of the Pondos, Pondomisis, Bacas, Xesibes, and others, were constantly fighting among themselves. She and her husband were residing at Buntingville. Faku was opposed to Mr. Jenkins preaching, for he said it would make his people cowards in fight and afraid of death if they were spoken too often about another world. Two years of famine followed after her arrival at Buntingville, during which the sufferings of the people were indescribable, but then good seasons came, the crops were abundant, and they rapidly recovered. Mr. Jenkins by this time had acquired the chief's confidence, and there seemed a good prospect of his being able to do a large work in the improvement of the tribe.

Of late years the principal Pondo chief has tried to ignore the treaty of 1844, but that treaty, or rather the policy of the Imperial Government of which it was the outcome, was the foundation of his tribe's present greatness and power. It was the establishment of the Republic of Natalia that gave Faku relief from Zulu inroads and an opportunity of recovering strength. But if that Republic had continued in existence he would have had only the district between the Umtata and the Umzimvubu. The Imperial Government might without any injustice have retained the last named river as the southern boundary of the Colony of Natal, instead of which it withdrew to the Umzimkulu, and surrendered to Faku all the intervening ground.

Then the treaty gave the Pondos prestige. Forty years ago the word "Government" was to the clan beyond the Orange and the Bashee what the word "Rome" was to the tribes along the Rhine and the Danube at the commencement of our era. It was a symbol of enormous strength, a mighty awe-inspiring spell. As the friend and ally of "Government" Faku had little difficulty in incorporating with his own people a great number of petty refugee clans, whose tendency was to gravitate towards any centre of real or supposed power.

Lastly, the treaty enriched the chief's family. Under it he received an annual subsidy of £75, apparently a very small sum but really an amount that enabled him in the course of a few years to become the owner of enormous herds of cattle.

In 1845, the year after the treaty, Mr. Jenkins founded a mission station on a site selected by Faku within a few miles of his birth place. Here Mr. Jenkins lived, exercising great influence with the Pondo chiefs, until 1867, when Faku died at the age of nearly ninety years. Mr. Jenkins survived him only four months. The widow of the missionary remained in the country, and until her death a few years ago exercised even greater influence in Pondoland than her husband had done.

In 1848 Mr. Henry F. Fynn was appointed British Resident with Faku. This officer was thoroughly acquainted with the condition and recent history of Kafirland, having lived for many years in Natal when Tshaka and Dingaan ruled that country. Like the other Europeans there at the time he had collected a number of destitute natives about him, who regarded him as their chief. In 1829 he incurred Dingaan's displeasure and was compelled to flee from Natal Bay, when he took refuge in a secluded valley a few miles east of the Umzimvubu near the sea coast. His village there was visited by Captain Gardiner, who marked its position in his map. Mr. Fynn afterwards entered the service of the Cape Government. As resident with Faku he acquired influence with the Pondos scarcely less than that of Mr. Jenkins. On one occasion, in 1850, Faku testified his regard for him by a present of a hundred head of cattle collected for the purpose among the different clans of the tribe. But soon after this the policy of the Imperial Government was changed, it was resolved to leave the natives as much as possible to themselves, and the Resident was withdrawn.

In 1850 the negotiations with Natal recorded in another chapter took place.

A few years later there was a project mooted of removing the bulk of the recent immigrant natives from Natal, and locating them under Mr. Theophilus Shepstone as Supreme Chief, on land to be obtained from Faku for that purpose. The object was to facilitate colonization, and the plan was the same as that adopted by the Emigrant Volksraad in 1841. Mr. Shepstone visited the Pondo country, May to August 1854, and obtained Faku's consent to his occupying such extent of ground as would be sufficient for his purpose, between Natal and the frontier Pondo kraals. At the same time Faku made over to Mr. Shepstone's exclusive control the mouth and port of the St. John's river. This arrangement was not carried out, but when Sir Philip Wodehouse located various refugee tribes in the territory now known as Griqualand East, the small district between the Umtamvuna and Umzimkulu rivers was with Faku's consent annexed to Natal.

From this time onwards the history of Pondoland is so closely connected with that of Griqualand East, the Xesibe district, and the Port of St. John's that the leading events have already of necessity been recorded in other papers.

Umqikela, Faku's son and successor, had never shown himself well disposed towards the Colony, he has much less ability than his father, is addicted to drunkenness, is intolerably vain, and has always been swayed by evil advisers, European and native. His conduct has more than once provoked hostilities and it has only been by the exercise of great forbearance that the Government has abstained from war. He has refused to surrender criminals, in accordance with the conditions of the treaty. He encouraged the Griqua insurgents by giving shelter to their leaders, permitted them to raise forces within his territory, and actually aided them with a contingent of ninety men under command of his nephew Josiah Jenkins. This contingent marched to Mt. Currie, encamped there with the rebels, and only surrendered to Captain Blyth when Josiah saw that resistance meant certain destruction. There can hardly be a doubt that he was secretly plotting with the Zulus in 1878.

Owing to this hostile course of action the Colonial Government considered it advisable to extend its jurisdiction over Eastern Pondoland, but the Imperial authorities objected to the occupation of the country. The recognition of Nquiliso as independent of Umqikela and the occupation of the Port of St. John's were, however, approved of.

Since that time the relationship between Umqikela and the Government of the Colony has remained in an unsatisfactory state, but there has been no open rupture. Nquiliso, son of Ndamasi and chief of Western Pondoland, has never given cause of complaint.

GEO. M. THEAL.

PORT OF ST. JOHN'S.

(BLUE BOOK ON NATIVE AFFAIRS 1885).

This name is applied to the mouth and tidal estuary of the St. John's river with both banks and a strip of land in extent about ten thousand acres or a little less than sixteen square miles on the western side above the sea.

The river called by us the St. John's, known to the natives as the Umzimvubu, that is "the place of residence of the hippotamus," has its rise in the Quathlamba mountains, and passes through Griqualand East and Pondoland in its course to the Indian Ocean. Its numerous tributaries, flowing through some of the richest land and most picturesque scenery in South Africa, drain a great extent of country. The mouth of the river, in common with all the streams along this coast, is unfortunately nearly closed by a shifting bar of sand. When heavy rains fall in the uplands a channel is sometimes opened across the bar thirty feet and upwards in depth at low water of spring tides, but on other occasions the channel is often not more than three feet deep. Above the bar a placid sheet of water from two hundred to two hundred and fifty yards across and from twenty to thirty feet in depth, extends some eleven or twelve miles, when a ford is reached.

For the last two miles of its course the river passes through an enormous rent in the elevated coast called the Gates of St. John. From the water rises on each side a sharply inclined bank covered with dark evergreen forest trees, above which frown sheer precipices of naked rock a thousand feet and upward in height. Above the Gates the river winds between rugged banks clothed with trees and grass, highly picturesque, but less grand than the stupendous cleft below.

There are other places along the coast where boats can effect a landing in fine weather, but the mouth of the St. John's is the only place worthy of the name of harbour between East London and Port Natal. The outer anchorage is fairly good, and the river is as accessible to boats, coasters and small steamers as is the Buffalo at East London. The greatest drawback to its use has been, not the difficulty of landing and shipping cargoes, but the difficulty of communicating with the back country, owing to the ruggedness of the land near the coast and the absence of anything like a waggon road.

It is evident that the control of the mouth of the St. John's must be considered a matter of supreme importance by the Colonial Government. Through it, if in unfriendly hands, goods could be conveyed to the interior without the payment of customs duties, firearms and ammunition might be supplied to all the natives of Kafirland. The river divides Pondoland into two nearly equal portions, and the Pondos alone could lay claim to the ground about its mouth. In 1844 the paramount Pondo chief Faku entered into a treaty with Sir Peregrine Maitland, in the 8th clause of which he agreed "that he would not suffer the masters or mariners of any ships or vessels to land merchantice, or to traffic with his people in any part of his country, unless such vessels should be furnished with a licence from the Colonial Government authorizing them to land goods there."

During the lifetime of Faku this clause of the treaty was not strictly observed. No foreign shipmaster attempted to enter the river, but a coasting trade was opened up by merchants in Natal, who made use of the port of St. John's without remonstrance from the Government of the Cape Colony.

In 1867 Faku died, leaving Umqikela, his great son, paramount chief of the Pondos, and Ndamasi, his son of the right hand, chief of the clans west of the St. John's. Practically Ndamasi was almost independent. It has indeed been asserted that Faku made him actually independent by promising that the Umsila* should never be sent across the river. It has been satisfactorily proved that no Umsila was sent from the Great chief's residence to any clan under Ndamasi's government for many years before Faku's death. On the other hand it is maintained that this was only a personal privilege given by Faku to his favourite son, and that it was not intended to indicate a division of the Pondo tribe. This is the view of the case taken by impartial natives, and the balance of Pondo evidence is greatly in its favour. At any rate the paramountcy of Umqikela meant very little more to Ndamasi than an admission that the son of the great house was of higher rank than his elder brother.

The Pondo tribe has incorporated so many alien clans that its division into two, or even into a dozen sections independent of each other, would not cause much difficulty. When Faku died Ndamasi was an old man with the reputation of being an intelligent chief, and Umqikela was only thirty-two years of age, and a drunkard and without any capacity as a ruler. Under these circumstances, Sir Philip Wodehouse, who wished to secure the mouth of the river for the Colony, applied personally to Ndamasi for it when he visited the country in 1869, but met with a distinct refusal.

On the 29th of August 1876 Ndamasi died. He was succeeded by his son Nquiliso, who was of about the same age as Umqikela. Nquiliso followed his father's policy in claiming independence of the great house in everything except an admission of its superior rank. Owing to his position he was more disposed to be friendly to the Colony than was Umqikela, who asserted his rights as paramount chief of the Pondo tribe in language such as James II. of England might have used, and with as little inclination as that monarch to adapt his conduct to the necessities of his time.

In 1878 the Government considered it imperative to obtain a firmer footing at the Port of St. John's. Umqikela, the chief of a tribe composed largely of alien clans ready at any moment to transfer their allegiance to someone else, with his authority actually ignored by a very large section of the tribe who claimed independence under another

---

* The *umsila* is the messenger who carries out the sentences of the chief. The word means "a tail," and the messenger is so called because he carries as a symbol of his authority the skin of the tail of a lion or leopard (in some tribes of an ox) stretched over a wand four or five feet long.

branch of the ruling house, could not be permitted to stand in the way
of the adoption of a policy that would affect all South Africa. It
cannot fairly be made a charge of injustice against the Government
that it did not support the pretensions of an unfriendly, incompetent
and drunken chief to an authority which he was altogether unable to
enforce.

On the 17th of July 1878 an agreement was made with Nquiliso by
Major Elliot for the Colonial authorities, whereby that chief ceded to
the Government of the Cape Colony all the sovereign rights which he
then possessed or was entitled to claim over the water and navigation
of the Umzimvubu, as also of a piece of land on which to erect a
custom house and other necessary buildings, such land to be paid for
at a fair valuation. He further agreed to roads being made and
maintained through the country on his side of the river from the port
to the main waggon road from the Cape Colony to Natal. On the
other part Nquiliso was acknowledged as independent of Umqikela,
from whose attacks he was promised protection as long as he
maintained friendly relations with the Government of the Cape of Good
Hope. This agreement was subsequently ratified by the Government,
and the Secretary for Native Affairs in person concluded it (on the 30th
of September) by paying to Nquiliso £1,000 for a narrow strip of land
on the western side of the river from the sea upwards about nine miles.

A few weeks subsequent to the arrangement between Major Elliot
and Nquiliso, General Thesiger, under the Governor's instructions,
proceeded from Port Natal to the St. John's mouth in Her Majesty's
ship Active. On the 31st of August 1878 he landed, hoisted the English
flag, and proclaimed the eastern bank of the river British territory
from the lower ford to the sea. The General was accompanied by
Major Crealock, Captain Harrison, Assistant Commissary General
Pennell, Lieut. Cameron, R.E., Lieut. Davis, R.N., and the Rev. J. O.
Oxland. A company of the first batallion of the 24th Regiment, ten
men of the Royal Engineers, and a detachment of blue jackets were
landed to witness the ceremony of hoisting and saluting the flag.
Major Elliot and five of Nquiliso's councillors were also witnesses of
the proceedings, though at a distance, for they were stationed on the
western bank of the river opposite the place where the ceremony was
performed.

A site was then sought for a fort. General Thesiger selected a spot
on the western bank close to the ford now known as Davis Drift. This
was about two miles above the strip of land which Nquiliso agreed to
sell, and his councillors who were present declared that they had no
power to cede it. Major Elliot thereupon proceeded to Nquiliso's
residence, but found the chief averse to disposing of the site selected
for the fort, as he stated he had promised the flat in which it was to
those of his subjects who would lose their gardens in the land already
sold. He had no objection, however, to its being occupied temporarily
by the troops. General Thesiger left there the Company of the 24th
under Captain Harrison and the Royal Engineers under Lieutenant

Cameron, and they remained until August 1879, when they were relieved by a company of the 99th Regiment. The fort was named by General Thesiger Fort Harrison. It was abandoned and dismantled in 1882, when the Cape Infantry then forming the garrison were moved down to the mouth of the river.

At the time of hoisting the flag, the highland on the western side of the mouth was named Mount Thesiger, and that on the eastern side was named Mount Sullivan.

On the 4th of September 1878 the High Commissioner completed the annexation of Port St. John's to the British dominions by the issue of a proclamation in which he enumerated the complaints against Umqikela, —knowingly harbouring criminals who had committed murder in British territory and refusing to deliver them up to justice, sheltering an insurgent Griqua leader for a time and then sending him home with an escort that assisted the rebels, general unfriendly and hostile conduct; he declined the offer of Umqikela to pay a fine of a thousand head of cattle; he declared that Umqikela would no longer be recognized as paramount chief of the Pondos, but that subordinate chiefs would be allowed to deal directly with the British Government; he declared further that Umqikela would not be permitted to exercise any control or authority over the navigation of the St. John's river, that the sovereignty over the port and tidal estuary of that river should be thenceforth vested in Her Majesty's Government, and that officers would be appointed on behalf of that Government to control its navigation and to levy any customs or port dues which it might be necessary to impose. In a notice of the same date it was announced that the customs duties would be the same as those of the Cape Colony.

The Imperial Government coincided with these measures. In a despatch dated the 13th of February 1879 Sir Michael Hicks Beach conveyed to Sir Bartle Frere "the approval of Her Majesty's Government to the establishment of British sovereignty over the port and tidal estuary of the St. John's river, and of the manner in which that measure has been carried out."

On the 10th October 1881 Letters Patent were issued under the Great Seal of the United Kingdom, empowering the Governor to issue a proclamation annexing Port St. John's to the Cape Colony as soon as an Act for that purpose should be passed by the Cape Parliament. Just before the close of the session of 1884, such an Act was brought forward by the Ministry. It was read in the House of Assembly for the first time on the 16th of July, read a second time and considered in committee on the 17th and read for the third time on the 18th. In the Legislative Council it passed through all its stages on the 18th of July. On the 15th of September 1884 the Governor issued a proclamation completing the annexation, since which date Port St. John's has been part of the Cape Colony and subject to all its laws.

The civil establishments have been as follows:

At the time of annexation to the Empire, Major Elliot and the Rev. J. O. Oxland were appointed British Residents respectively in Western and Eastern Pondoland. Each of these officers held a commission under the Imperial Act 26 and 27 Victoria c. 35. On the 19th of November 1878 Mr. H. M. Edye assumed duty as Magistrate and Sub Collector of Customs at the Port. He had a clerk to assist him. In February 1882 Mr. Edye was removed and Mr. Oxland was required to perform the combined duties of British Resident in Eastern Pondoland and Magistrate and Sub Collector of Customs at Port St. John's. In September 1884 the office of British Resident in Eastern Pondoland was abolished, and Captain Whindus succeeded Mr. Oxland as Magistrate. In October 1878 Mr. T. R. Bangay was appointed Harbour Master and Pilot, and he continued to fill those offices from the date of his arrival (19th November 1878) until September 1884, when they were abolished. The Magistrate is now also Port Captain and Shipping Master, and there is a separate Custom House Officer.

The population of the annexed territory in September 1884 consisted of 308 souls, viz. : 110 officers and men of the Cape Infantry, 92 European officials and traders with their families, and 106 native servants. No ground has yet been disposed of to private individuals, but several substantial buildings have been erected at various points in the territory.

The trade of Port St. John's to the present time has been very small, the waggon road to Umtata being not yet completed. Most of the goods imported come from Natal in small coasting steamers. The exports consist chiefly of hides, horns, and maize. The customs duties collected were in 1879 £499, in 1880 £1,745, in 1881 £1,593, in 1882 £2,251, in 1883 £2,120, and in 1884 £1,963.

GEO. M. THEAL.

Native Affairs Office, January 1885.

HISTORIC SKETCH OF THE TRIBES ANCIENTLY INHABITING THE COLONY OF NATAL AS AT PRESENT BOUNDED—AND ZULULAND.

(Appendix to Proceedings of Commission on Native Laws and Customs 1883).

1. Towards the close of the last century, the two countries at present known as the Colony of Natal and Zululand, were thickly inhabited by numerous Native tribes closely located together, intermarrying with each other, and living generally in terms of peace and friendship; they possessed cattle, sheep and a small kind of goat, and cultivated the soil, from which they mainly drew their subsistence.

2. Each tribe had its own Chief, who although ruling as a sort of patriarch, possessed and exercised the power of life and death. In those days, domestic quarrels were more frequent than inter-tribal ones; arising mostly out of disputes about succession between members of the Chief's families.

3. Tribal quarrels of course also occurred, in some cases periodically; but the wars arising out of them seldom lasted longer than a few days; or as the natives describe it, "an army never slept away from its home," and never, within the territory now known as the Colony of Natal, did war cause the destruction of a tribe; one battle, such as it was, usually terminated the dispute; and it not unfrequently happened, that young warriors whose addresses had been paid to girls of the tribe with which they had been fighting, sent home their shields from the field of battle by their friends, and returned with their late foes to prosecute their love suits; the lives of women and children were respected, prisoners taken in battle were not put to death, but detained till ransomed; and victory, rather than plunder and devastation, seems to have been the great object of these encounters.

4. In none of the tribes was there at that time any military organisation, nor the least sign of aggressive ambition. The Umtetwa was one of the most considerable tribes in the country now called Zululand, and occupied the lower part of the Black and White Imfolozi Rivers; Jobe was its chief. The Zulus were then an inconsiderable tribe occupying only a small portion of the upper basin of the White Imfolozi River and were tributary to the Umtetwa from whom they were separated by one or two small tribes also tributary to the Umtetwa Chief. Senzangakona, Chaka's father, was chief over the Zulus; the more immediate independent neighbours of the Umtetwa power, were Zwide, Chief of the Amandwandwa tribe, Matiwana of the Amangwana tribe, Goza of the Abatembu, Macingwane of the Amacunu, to the North, West, and South.

5. The Umtetwa chief, Jobe, had two sons, Tana and Godongwana, and as old age approached, he determined to make timely arrangements for the succession, he appointed Tana, the elder of the two, as his heir, and assigned to him one of the royal kraals as a residence; the young man, however, became impatient, and with his younger brother plotted against their father's life; this was discovered and the old Chief ordered both of them to be put to death; he especially directed that the younger, believed by him to be the most ambitious and dangerous of the two, should not escape; an armed party

surrounded the hut the two young men were in during the night, and every man found in it was put to death on the spot, including Tana the elder son; Godongwana, however, escaped through the doorway and leaped the outer fence, but in doing so received a double barbed assegai in his back; he fled to the bush and concealed himself, but was sought for and discovered next day by his sister, who extracted the assegai, and gave him food as well as a particular kaross; search was afterwards made for him by his father's directions, but by disguising one of his attendants with his sister's robe and other means, he escaped out of his father's country.

6. It is remarkable that these events in the personal history of Godongwana, led to all the great changes in the habits, condition and destiny of the immense native population, occupying almost from the Zambesi to the St. John's River, and may be said to have caused Natal to become a British Colony.

7. It was probably in 1785-90, that Godongwana escaped from the fate intended by his father: badly wounded and reported to be dead, he wandered from tribe to tribe; stories of miraculous escapes are related of him, and eventually he found his way far enough South to come in contact with white people; he studied the habits and mode of warfare of his new acquaintances, perhaps as a servant, and at length returned after the death of his father, to his own tribe; he had acquired two horses, and came back to his people "sitting upon one of them;" in those days a horse was an unknown animal in the present Natal and Zululand, and the romantic descriptions forwarded to his tribe of the young chief himself, and the animal upon which he rode, added prestige to the rightful claim he possessed to the power of his father; his approach was slowly and cautiously made; circumstances such as these, secured for him a superstitious reverence from the people, and the scar of the wound he had received, served to identify him as the lost son; the reigning chief fled with a portion of the people, but Godongwana eventually overcame him and put him to death; he met with opposition from some of his father's tributaries, but he at length, made himself undisputed master of the Umtetwa power; in compliment to his wonderful history, his name was changed and he became afterwards celebrated under the name of "Dingiswayo," which means "The Wanderer" or he who was caused to wander.

8. Dingiswayo no sooner found himself firmly established as Chief, than he introduced among his people the principles of military organisation which he had learnt from the white people during his wanderings. It is difficult to judge how long his exile lasted, but the probabilities are that it must have been ten to fifteen years.

9. Not long after the return of Godongwana, now Dingiswayo events happened in the Zulu country, which were destined to carry to its utmost extent, the great revolution commenced by Dingiswayo's introduction of the new military system among his people.

10. Senzangakona the Chief of the small tributary Zulu tribe, had an illegitimate son named Chaka, born to an accidental intimacy with

a girl of the Elangeni tribe. The young man was energetic and talented and assumed airs which gave offence to the Chief's family; and in consequence of their hostility, he and his mother were compelled to fly for their lives, and took refuge with Dingiswayo, one of whose regiments he entered as a private soldier; this in all probability occurred about 1805. Chaka accompanied his regiment in all Dingiswayo's expeditions and earned for himself a great military reputation.

11. Dingiswayo never allowed women and children to be put to death, and frequently released them when they had been taken prisoners; he cared little for the capture of cattle, and thought that the greatest evidence of victory, was to quarter his army in his enemy's country; he made a rule of doing this so long as there was grain enough to support it, to be found belonging to a defeated tribe. The consequence was, that he never utterly destroyed or permanently dispersed any people with whom he went to war; they usually re-occupied their country and acknowledged Dingiswayo as their paramount Chief, until it suited them to do otherwise.

12. Chaka disapproved of this policy, because he thought it would ultimately lead to dangerous combinations against the Supreme Chief; he thought that the only safe plan was to inflict such an injury as would thoroughly disorganise; hence, when he acquired power he adopted the uncompromising system which raised the Zulu power to such renown in South Africa.

13. After Chaka had served long enough in Dingiswayo's army, to master the system introduced by that chief, and to mark the defects of it, his father Senzangakona died, and he became the Chief of the Zulus about 1810; by this time all the neighbouring tribes had been compelled in self-defence, to adopt the new military system, and among others, Zwide, chief of the most powerful neighbouring native tribe, had done so extensively; between this chief and Dingiswayo, many battles took place, Dingiswayo more than once occupied Zwide's country with his army until he had exhausted all its stores of corn, and had several times taken Zwide prisoner, and as often released him, because, he said he was only fighting to show the superiority of his army, and Zwide was the companion of his father. On one occasion, however, Dingiswayo, was with a small guard, too much in advance of his own army, and was himself captured by Zwide;—perhaps about 1818,—the latter wished to emulate the generosity of his former conqueror and release him, but the counsels of his mother Tombazi prevailed, and Dingiswayo was put to death; his army was soon after defeated and his country overrun by Zwide's forces, when the Umtetwa tribe took refuge under Chaka; from that time to the present day, they have continued to form a portion of the Zulu power, although they have retained their separate tribal name.

14. But before this disastrous termination to the Umtetwa power, Dingiswayo, its chief, had been in the habit of calling upon Chaka as his vassal, to co-operate with him in expeditions against any of his more formidable neighbours whom he wished to subdue, and one of them is

notable from its having been made on the Amangwane, a numerous
tribe residing in the North-Western part of the present Zululand, about
1819. The Amangwane were defeated and compelled to retire to the
South-West, but they were strong enough to overcome other tribes in
their way, and to reimburse their losses by the booty they took from
them in passing through their country, they entered what is the present
Colony of Natal, in the Division of Newcastle, and settled themselves
under the Drakensberg, where Zikali, the son of the chief Matiwana,
now resides with the same tribe. Some years after, they were again
attacked by Chaka and driven to what is now called the Orange Free
State, Moshesh became their tributary, until again driven by one of
Chaka's expeditions, when they crossed once more to the coast face of
the Drakensberg, towards the Frontier tribes of the Cape Colony;
their approach caused great alarm, and a Colonial force acting with
that of the Frontier Kafirs, encountered and defeated them so completely, as to induce the chief Matiwane to resolve on returning to
offer his allegiance to Chaka, as a subject, Chaka had however in the
meantime been assassinated, and Matiwana, although received with
every mark of kindness by Dingaan, Chaka's successor, was soon after
put to death by him because he feared his genius.

15. The entrance of this tribe into what is now the Colony of Natal,
was the first shock felt by its unwarlike inhabitants, from the military
spirit and new tactics which had unknown to them, been growing up in
the East; this was however the effect of the combined action of the
Umtetwa power under Dingiswayo and the small Zulu force under
Chaka; all the subsequent attacks upon this tribe were made by Chaka
alone.

16. When Chaka became chief over both the Umtetwas and Zulus,
after the death of Dingiswayo, he found himself strong enough to
undertake short aggressive expeditions; the immediate neighbourhood
of Zwide the conqueror of Dingiswayo, rendered it imprudent for him
to go far, or to take the whole of his force from home, but he was
nevertheless enabled to force the Amacunu and Abatembu tribe, then
residing on the lower Buffalo or Umzimyati and Tugela Rivers,
principally on the left bank, to move to the South for their safety; both
these were numerous aud powerful, and their retreat was through the
centre of what is now the Colony of Natal, and formed the second and
third wave which swept over its inhabitants, who although occasionally
attempting a combined resistance, were defeated and dispersed; they
were no match for Chaka's neighbours, rendered formidable by having
adopted more or less of the new military system. In the retreat of
these two tribes, they interfered with and unsettled all the country
inland of the parallel of Pietermaritzburg to the Drakensberg; and by
their departure and the vanquishing and incorporation by Chaka of the
Amacube, and neighbouring tribes, all barriers were removed between
this dreaded chief and the tribes of and to the South of the Tugela
valley, including the present Colony of Natal.

17. But for some time after the commencement of his career. Chaka
had too formidable a near neighbour to feel himself safe enough to
undertake any distant enterprise; Zwide the conqueror of Dingiswayo

was at hand and prudence compelled Chaka to be on his guard. Zwide made several attacks upon him and at length compelled him to evacuate his country and retreat to the Tugela valley; Zwide's army followed him, but he could not cope with Chaka as a general, was out-manoeuvred and defeated in battle;—Chaka promptly followed up his advantage and compelled him and a portion of his people to fly his country; the great majority of Zwide's people then submitted to Chaka and became Zulu subjects, and the last serious check upon Chaka's victorious career was then removed.

18. The tribes of the Tugela valley and the numerous ones of the present Colony of Natal now became next neighbours to the Zulus; those living in the valley, possessed the advantage of the shelter of the extensive valley jungle, and several of them were allowed by Chaka to occupy their lands as tributary, on their promptly tendering their submission to him; others were attacked and driven further South one, the Amakabela, although repeatedly attacked, and reduced to live upon roots and wild animals, perseveringly clung to their ancient homes, and in spite of all the vicissitudes of those eventful times remained in the occupation of their country; sometimes as persecuted fugitives, living in rocks and bushes; at others, as vassals of some tribe more favoured by the ruling power; and they still occupy the land of their forefathers, under their present chief Magedama, who with his tribe became British subjects on the proclamation of Natal as a British Colony.

19. The numerous Natal tribes, not inhabiting the Tugela valley, and situated below or on the coast side of the parallel, disturbed by the three retreating waves already noticed, soon found themselves exposed to the full brunt of Zulu attack; those more immediately opposite the seat of Zulu power, that is between thirty-five to sixty-five miles from the sea, felt it most; but none were strong enough singly, to force themselves through the tribes in their rear and avoid, as others had done for the time, the attack of the Zulus; with this difficulty behind and Chaka in front, their only course was to form a confederacy strong enough to overbear all opposition and move to the South; they succeeded, and carried with them the Amabaca and other tribes next below the course of the Amatembu and Amacunu already described; and thus a fresh belt of inhabitants was disturbed and dispossessed, by a fourth wave put in motion by the advance of the military system introduced by Dingiswayo;—this occurred about 1814.

20. It was the universal terror caused by this system, that so completely changed the sentiment and acts of tribes hitherto friendly to each other; consideration of self-preservation led friend to turn upon friend; all ancient alliances and friendships melted away before the new circumstances; first tribes, then families became disorganised, until at length almost every man's hand was turned against his neighbour. Those tribes who were accepted by the universal enemy Chaka as his tributaries, became aggressors in proportion to their strength, in imitation and with the support of their master. In addition

to the minor forays by these, the country was traversed by the organised Zulu forces, whose orders were, to exterminate man, woman and child, and bring home their cattle as the property of the King. Chaka's policy seemed to have been to annually widen the circle of devastation around him, so that every year his expeditions became more distant, until at length they crossed the St. John's River on the South, and King George's on the North. Those tribes who in his early career evaded him by passing to the South, were subsequently overtaken by his forces, in their new homes, and either dispersed or destroyed; three only of the many who came in contact with him, escaped destruction at his hands, namely, *first*,—the Abatembu, who attempted to expel the Amapondo under Faku, from their country, but were defeated and their Chief killed in battle by Faku; *second*,—the Amagwana under Matiwana, who attempted to occupy the country of some of the Frontier tribes, and were met, defeated in battle and dispersed, by the Cape Colonial and Frontier Tribal Forces; and *third*,—the Amabaca under Madikane who came into contact with the Tambookies, a Cape Frontier tribe, by whom they were defeated, their chief killed, and the tribe driven back.

21. The course of Chaka's conquest to the South was checked by the existence of the Colony of the Cape of Good Hope, and on the North by the attacks of fever and a kind of cholera, which caused great mortality among his army in the low country about St. George's River.

22. Chaka always felt great respect for the English power, and wished to be on good terms with the Cape Colony, probably from what he had heard from the wanderer Dingiswayo, and from knowing that the system which had made him so successful in war, had been introduced from that Colony.

23. But the conditions of the territory now known as Natal, became every year more deplorable; annually traversed by Zulu armies, aided by the constant forays of tributaries, no tribe could re-organise itself; cultivation of the soil became dangerous, because scarcity of food was universal, and hungry wanderers invariably destroyed the cultivators, and were in turn themselves destroyed by other, but stronger parties, as hungry as they; at length cultivation ceased altogether, and famine caused the loss of more life than the assegai.

24. The only domestic animals left to these wretched people, were their dogs, and with the assistance of these they succeeded occasionally in capturing game, but as the urgent demands of hunger seldom suffered these animals to share in the meal they captured, they soon became useless from starvation, and at length formed the only animal food with which the wild roots were flavoured by their masters; wolves became so daring from constantly feeding on human flesh, that they boldly attacked men and women, and continually carried off children. The country became filled with small parties of starving and desperate men; there was but one step to cannibalism, and this was soon taken by a man named Umdava, who conceived the idea of eating human flesh, and a considerable band soon gathered round him;

his example was followed by others, until the fragments of four tribes had become cannibals; they hunted for human beings as men do for game, and became a far more terrible scourge to the country than Chaka's armies. I have myself conversed with several men, who escaped after having been captured by these "man-eaters," and after having been told off to furnish the next feast of their captors; and with one, a chief still living in this Colony, who was compelled to carry the vessel in which he was told he would himself be cooked; the scene of his escape is not five miles from the spot on which this paper is written, and at present forms part of the episcopal property held by the Bishop of Natal.

25. Perishing from famine, harassed by fierce wolves and still fiercer cannibals, the scattered population at length turned their attention to the Zulu country, where, whatever might be the government, they could at least get food; and thousands of individuals presented themselves, destitute and starving, to be "picked up" by the Zulus.

26. The effect of Chaka's operations was to destroy all security of life, and to make his government attractive in comparison with the misery it caused to those without its pale; but even in spite of all this suffering, many individuals and sections of tribes, preferred to brave out the storm, in forests and other places of concealment, to placing themselves in the power of one so much dreaded.

27. The large tribes who had been the first to disturb the aboriginal inhabitants of Natal, in their endeavours to pass through the country now known by that name, to escape from Chaka, having been overtaken and dispersed by Chaka's armies in their new residences, and their chiefs mostly killed, now found further flight useless, and the great body of their population returned and became subjects to the Zulu King, who distributed them among his head men and chief officers and incorporated the young men into his army as soldiers; and it is remarkable that such of these three tribes as entered Natal in 1812 or 1813, for the first time as fugitives from Chaka, and who afterwards returned and became Zulu subjects, now occupy as British subjects, almost the same tracts of country they settled upon when they first entered the territory.

28. They with several others are ranked in a different class from the aboriginal inhabitants, because although they occupied part of this country long before any white settlement was thought of, they were not among the more ancient of the inhabitants.

29. Those tribes, however, who as soon as they found out Chaka's policy and power, tendered their submission and allegiance to him and were accepted as tributaries, were the Amabomvu, the Amanxamalala, the Abambo, the Amakabela, the Amancolosi, the Amacele, and others; they occupied the valley of the Tugela, from its junction with the Buffalo or Umzinyati River, to the sea and along the coast to the Tongati River.

30. Towards the latter part of his reign, Chaka moved one of the royal kraals called "Dukuza," across the Tugela to the Umvoti River, into what is now Natal; from this he marched his last expedition

against the Amampondo, whom he defeated, and captured large numbers of their cattle, but did not disperse; Faku their chief, sent a deputation to follow the army on its return and tender his submission to Chaka.

31. On the Zulu army reaching home, it was ordered to proceed to the North, on another expedition, without taking rest; and shortly after its re-departure, the King was assassinated by his brothers at his own residence, in what is now Natal, and in the full career of his success, on the 23rd of September, 1828, in about the 41st year of his age.

32. It is said that Chaka met his death while giving audience to this Amapondo deputation, that he had accepted their submission, and had arranged with them for Lieutenant Farewell to receive part of the Amampondo country as a gift from himself, in lieu of part of the neighbourhood of Port Natal, which was what Farewell wanted.

33. By such events as those described above was the territory now called Natal depopulated, and the Zulu power built up; to avoid starvation and the other horrors of insecurity, the people became Zulus, and Natal was transformed from a thickly settled and universally cultivated peaceful country, to a wilderness, in which the remnants of its inhabitants were almost universally killing or being killed.

34. Chaka was succeeded by Dingaan, his brother and assassinator; at that time the Zulus and their tributaries occupied the present Zulu country, and both banks of the Tugela River from Job's Kop to the sea, and southward along the coast as far as the Umgeni, and the King's cattle kraals extended to the south bank of the Umzimkulu River.

35. The tributary tribes which had been allowed by Chaka to retain their own chiefs and internal government down the valley of the Tugela, and which still retained these at his death, had enjoyed from their position along the valley, the greatest facilities for strengthening themselves, by acquiring additional population from the scattered inhabitants of the dispersed tribes, because the refugees reached them first.

36. Four years before Chaka's death, some Europeans had settled at Port Natal, and around these men was also congregated a considerable population belonging to the dispersed tribes, to whom desertion from the Zulus became frequent.

37. On Dingaan's accession, symptoms of disaffection showed themselves in various parts of the Zulu country; some tribes revolted and moved off to the northward; Qeto the surviving chief of the Amaqwabe tribe, took the opportunity of moving to the South, along the coast; in his course he took possession of the King's cattle, he was followed by a Zulu force, but he defeated it and turned freebooter; it was he who treacherously murdered Messrs. Farewell and Thackwray and party, on the St. John's River, on their return from the Cape with goods for Chaka; he was however soon after totally defeated in an attack he made upon Faku, his power was completely broken, and he became a fugitive with his family; he reached one of the remnants of the Natal

tribes under Baleni, who upon reporting his arrival to Dingaan, was ordered to put him to death, and obeyed. It is necessary to explain that by this time most of the Natal population had actually been incorporated with the Zulus, and that the remnants who preferred not living immediately under Zulu rule, had found it safest to acknowledge the Zulu King, by paying some periodical tribute in feathers or skins, by these means their condition was much ameliorated.

38. These signs of disaffection caused much anxiety to the King Dingaan, who finding that the tributary chiefs had acquired so much strength, and fearing a combination against his power, determined to cut them off in detail, and appoint officers of his own to rule over their respective tribes; he succeeded in carrying out this policy to its fullest extent, and by drafting all their young men into his army he so completely amalgamated these tribes in his own government, that such members of the several chiefs' families as escaped being put to death, concealed their rank and passed as commoners. Finding also that the presence of European settlers at Port Natal was a great temptation to the Zulus to desert, and that there was great difficulty in recovering the deserters, he ordered the withdrawal of his people living to the South of the Tongati River, to the north of the river, and ultimately to the north bank of the Tugela, for 45 miles from its mouth.

39. It appears that the white settlers were on one occasion prevailed upon by threats of expulsion, and by promises of sparing the lives of the refugees, to give up a party of four, who in spite of those promises were immediately put to death; after this all refugees from the Zulu country were sent further south as soon as they reached the white settlers, when of course every attempt to discover them was ineffectual. Dingaan was evidently alarmed at the tendency of this, and about the year 1833, sent a force against the whites, from which they and their people escaped into the Amapondo country, and although most of the whites returned, many of the natives remained away until the presence of the Boers in 1837-38, afforded them sufficient protection against their old enemy.

40. The arrival in Natal of the emigrant Boers in 1837-1838, introduced an entirely new element into the politics of the country; and it will not be necessary to enter further into the history of that migration than is sufficient to show its effect upon the native population. When these emigrants came, they found the subjects of Dingaan, King of the Zulus, occupying the whole of the upper part of the Tugela valley, including the lower parts of the Mooi, Bushman's, Sunday's and Buffalo Rivers, down as far as the Krans Kop, or the present Fort Buckingham; while from that point to the sea, the left bank of the Tugela only was occupied, because the inhabitants on the right bank had been removed by Dingaan's order to prevent the facility for desertion to the European settlers which their presence naturally afforded.

41. Difficulties between the Boers and Dingaan occurred immediately on their first communications with each other, and these were soon increased to the extent of deadly hostility, by the treacherous murder of Retief and his party at Dingaan's kraal; as the struggle progressed,

the cause of the Boers was assisted by the revolt of the King's brother Panda, who joined them in the present Colony of Natal with fully half of the Zulu population.

42. This change in the state of parties soon decided the contest; the force brought through by Panda, fought for the Boers against Dingaan, who was defeated and compelled to fly, and was ultimately killed by the Amaswazi, a hostile native power to the north, Panda who with some of his councillors was kept in the Boers' camp as a precaution against treachery, was proclaimed King of the Zulus and at once assumed the government.

43. A portion of the people who originally accompanied him into the Colony on his revolt, went back with him; but a large portion, although they had fought on his side and had contributed to his being made King, refused to do so, they preferred the protection of the Boers to being any longer Zulu subjects.

44. These are the 100,000 people referred to by Mr. Commissioner Cloete, in his letters of the 10th November, 1843, and 10th August, 1848, as the large influx of "Refugees," which took place about 1839; it is however now shown beyond doubt, that they were the aboriginal inhabitants of the country, embracing the first opportunity that had offered itself to them, of occupying their ancient homes, without being subject to Zulu rule, and in all probability amounted to more than 100,000.

45. The rapidity with which events succeeded each other, prevented many from joining their respective tribes at the time; so that migration from the Zulu country, of individuals and families connected with these tribes, was very considerable for several years after Panda became King.

46. It is but natural to suppose that before he had completed his arrangements for checking this migration, it must have been much greater than after; opportunities would become more seldom and the risk greater when such arrangements were made; such was the case, and there are to this day, aboriginal inhabitants of this Colony, still living in the Zulu country, some from want of opportunity to join their relatives here, others from choice.

47. Thus we find that in 1812, the date when the inhabitants of the territory now called Natal, first began to be disturbed by the growth of the Zulu power, that territory was occupied by no less than ninety-four (94) separate tribes enumerated under Table No. 1, whose population must have been very numerous.

48. That forty-three (43) of these aboriginal tribes are now residing in Natal, still as separate as they originally were, that many members of them now living are the very individuals who formed part of the communities enumerated, before they were disturbed, and are living witnesses of the truth of this record, while the rest are, as a rule, the descendants of those communities.

49. That several of those aboriginal tribes who migrated to the South, such as the very considerable ones of the Amabele, the Amazizi and others, are at present among the people called Fingos, in the

Frontier Districts of the Cape Colony; and that three, the Amavundhle, the Abashwau and the Amabaca, occupy the territory called "No Man's Land," to the south of Natal, while a section of the Amabaca are in Natal; a fourth, the Amaxesibe, now live on the border of "No Man's Land."

50. That thirty-nine of the aboriginal tribes were so completely dispersed and their reigning families annihilated, that they no longer exist as separate tribes, but some of the individuals belonging to them congregated and formed others,—not under hereditary chiefs,—such as the Amaduma, and those enumerated under Table II Class No. 2; and that others have become incorporated with these aboriginal communities.

51. That there are seven tribes, enumerated under Class No. 3, of Table II, which entered the territory now the Colony of Natal, between 1812 and 1840-43, and were found here on its becoming a British Colony.

52. That there are six tribes or sections of tribes, enumerated under Class No. 4 Table II, some of which entered the Colony, from the effects of political convulsions since 1843, but of several of these it must be explained that portion of their population were in the Colony previous to the date assigned, but they formed either part of the general population, or were attached to other tribes settled in the Colony and remained so until the arrival of some member of their ancient reigning families, around whom they congregated; so that in some cases the chief followed the people, and the date of the chief's entering the Colony, has become that of the arrival of the tribe; it is difficult to discriminate between individuals of a tribe, many will therefore rank as having arrived after 1843, who were here before, and the reverse.

53. All the information upon which the foregoing sketch is based, has been obtained from natives who were actors in the scenes described; the particulars embrace a short sketch of the special history of each tribe, showing its ancient residence and fate; the only points not obtained from such information are the actual date of the death of Chaka, and his probable age.

T. SHEPSTONE,
Secretary for Native Affairs.

Office of the Secretary for Native Affairs,
   Pietermaritzburg, Natal, January 18, 1864.

THE MAITLAND TREATY.

TREATY OF AMITY entered into between His Excellency Lieutenant-General Sir Peregrine Maitland, Knight Commander of the Most Honourable Military Order of the Bath, of the Royal Military Order of William of the Netherlands, and of the Imperial Order of Saint Waldimer of Russia, Colonel of Her Majesty's 17th Regiment of Foot, Governor and Commander-in-Chief of Her Majesty's Castle, Town, and Settlement of the Cape of Good, in South Africa, and of the Territories and Dependencies thereof, and Ordinary and Vice-Admiral of the same, Commanding the Forces, etc., etc., etc., on behalf of Her Britannic Majesty, of the one part, and Faku, Paramount Chief of the Amapondo Nation, of the other part.

ARTICLE I. There shall be peace and amity for ever between Her Britannic Majesty and her subjects and Faku, the Paramount Chief of the Amapondo nation, and his subjects, and Faku promises that he will continue to be the faithful friend of the Colony of the Cape of Good Hope, and of all good subjects of Her Majesty.

2. The contracting Chief will not permit his subjects to harass or annoy the subjects of Her Majesty the Queen of England, who may pass through his country, or reside in it, with his permission, or who may be located in any British territory near the boundary of his country.

3. The contracting Chief will use his best exertions to seize and deliver up to the nearest British authority, for trial according to law, all persons who shall have committed, or shall be reasonably suspected to have committed, any murder, robbery or other offence within the limits of the Colony, or any of its parts or dependencies, and who shall be found in the territory of the said Chief.

4. Refugees and banditti belonging to other tribes, accused or suspected of having committed crimes within British territory, against the persons or properties of British subjects, and who may have fled in order to escape punishment, shall find no hiding place in Faku's country; but, on the contrary, Faku engages that he will use his best exertions to seize all such persons, and deliver them up to the nearest British authority, in order that they may be tried, and, if guilty, punished.

5. The contracting Chief undertakes to use his authority and influence to cause all persons within his territory, whose evidence may be required by any court of justice in any British territory in South Africa, to appear at the time and place prescribed; and he will take care, as much as possible, when delivering up any prisoner to any British authority, to produce, at the same time, to such authority, all witnesses acquainted with the matter in question, whose presence he can command or procure. The British Government, on the other hand, will be prepared to pay all witnesses who shall attend any such court as has been mentioned a reasonable compensation for their time and trouble.

6. All cattle, horses, or other property, stolen in any British territory in South Africa, and traced into the territory of the contracting Chief, shall, if found therein, be restored on demand of any proper

British authority, together with full compensation for the entire value of whatever property not found shall yet be proved to have been stolen at the same time; and in case none of the stolen property traced into the Chief's territory shall be found therein, then full compensation shall be made for all the property so traced.

7. All British subjects travelling between the territory of the Cape of Good Hope and Port Natal, with their servants and attendants, and also the native postmen or others employed in the transmission of letters, shall, at all times, be protected by the Chief, and permitted to pursue their journey without hindrance or molestation.

8. All British subjects resorting temporarily to his country, or residing therein by permission of the Chief, for purposes of trade or otherwise, shall be protected by him in their persons and property; but he will not suffer the masters or mariners of any ships or vessels to land merchandise, or to traffic with his people in any part of his country, unless such vessel shall be furnished with a licence from the Colonial Government, authorising them to land goods there.

9. The contracting Chief, having, many years ago, invited and received into his country Christian missionaries, for the instruction of his nation, hereby gives his true word and promise that he will continue to be the friend of the missionaries; that he will protect the persons, families, and property of all persons engaged as Christian teachers in his country; that he will permit any of his subjects who desire it to settle at or near any of the missionary villages or institutions within his territory, and to take their property there with them; that he will not allow any native Christian or inhabitant of a missionary village to be disturbed or injured in his person, family, or property, for refusing to comply with the customs touching witchcraft, rainmaking, polygamy, circumcision, and forcible abduction and violation of females; and that he will encourage his people to cause the regular attendance of their children at the Christian schools, that they may be taught to read the word of God, and be gradually trained to become a civilised community.

10. The contracting Chief, wishing to live in peace, hereby gives his true word and promise that he will, as far as possible, avoid making war on any of the tribes by whom he is surrounded; and, to that end, that he will endeavour to settle his disputes with other chiefs by peaceful methods; and if, in any case, his just rights and privileges shall be violated, and the offending chiefs refuse to give redress, he will call upon the Colonial Government to mediate between him and the other chiefs, so that war may, if possible, be prevented.

11. The contracting Chief, as the faithful friend of the Colonial Government, will be ready at all times, when called upon by that Government, to aid and assist the Colony with all his captains and warriors in any enterprise which may be necessary for the protection of the Colony, or the promotion of the general welfare and security.

12. The Governor of the Colony of the Cape of Good Hope, knowing that for many years past the contracting Chief has been a faithful friend of the subjects of Her Britannic Majesty, hereby gives his word and promise that the British Government will continue its friendship and favour towards Faku, the paramount Chief of the Amapondo nation, so long as he remains a faithful friend of the Colony; and as a proof of his friendship, the Governor, admitting the rightful claim long since made by Faku, hereby acknowledges that he is the paramount Chief of the whole territory lying betwixt the Umtata River from its mouth to the Waterfall Wagonford, thence along the ancient line of boundary between the Amapondo and Tambookie nations to the Kahlamba Mountain on the west; and the Umzimkulu, from its mouth along the principal western branch to its source in the Kahlamba Mountains on the east; and from the coast inland to a line to be drawn along the base of the Kahlamba range of mountains, between the sources of the said rivers.

13. The British Government will secure this territory to the contracting Chief against all claims or pretensions on the part of British subjects; but the rights of all petty chiefs and native tribes who have at any period heretofore resided upon any part of the said territory remain unaltered, and they will be at liberty to reside within the said territory in the same manner as they did before they were disturbed by the wars with the Zoolah nation.

14. The British Government will also afford to the contracting Chief as much aid and assistance as possible, in order to protect the Amapondo nation from unjust and unprovoked aggressions, and to enable the contracting Chief to fulfil his engagements entered into by this treaty.

15. The Colonial Government engages that it will cause its best efforts to be made to apprehend any persons residing at the time within any part of the colonial territories in South Africa, whether British subjects or otherwise, who have committed, or are reasonably suspected to have committed, any crime against the persons or property of the subjects of Faku, within his territory, and to deliver them up, to be dealt with according to the laws of the Colony, and to be tried in the Colony, and will use its influence and authority to cause all persons residing within the said territories, whether British subjects or otherwise, whose evidence may be required upon such cases, to appear at the time and place prescribed, and will cause all such witnesses to be paid a reasonable remuneration for their time and trouble in attending to give their evidence.

16. The Colonial Government further engages, as a mark of friendship, to cause an annual present of useful articles, or money, to the amount of seventy-five pounds sterling, per annum, to be made to the Chief Faku, so long as he continues to observe the terms of this treaty and to remain the faithful friend of the Colony.

This done at Fort Beaufort, this Seventh day of October, in the year of Our Lord One Thousand Eight Hundred and Forty-four.

(Signed) P. MAITLAND, Governor.

Signed and sealed in our presence:

JOHN MONTAGUE, Secretary to Government,
J. MOORE CRAIG.

This done at Faku's residence, this Twenty-third day of November, in the Year of Our Lord One Thousand Eight Hundred and Forty-four.

Marks of × FAKU, Paramount Chief,
„ „ × DAMAS, Chief's principal son.

Signed and sealed in our presence:

T. SHEPSTONE, Resident Diplomatic Agent to the Slambie Tribes,
W. M. D. Fynn, Resident Diplomatic Agent, to the Amacaleka Tribe,
THOMAS JENKINS, Wesleyan Missionary.

UMCIWENGI,	×,	Faku's brother,
BANGAZITA,	×,	Faku's son,
CINGO,	×,	Faku's brother,
UMVINJELWA,	×.	Councillor.

MEMO. ON MR. OXLAND'S REPORT OF 5TH OCTOBER TO SECRETARY FOR NATIVE AFFAIRS, REPORTING MEETING WITH UMQIKELA AND PONDOS.

(Return Relative to the Disturbance in Pondoland in 1880.)

Maritzburg, 13th November, 1878.

Mr. Oxland has put the matter so plainly and politely before the Pondos, showing what their position is, and has been, in reference to us, and what the conditions of the Treaty of 1844 implied, that it is unnecessary for me to add anything on this head. Faku, by his treaty obligations, relinquished the right of taking up arms against any of the numerous clans and petty chiefs who were then under his control, or who were by this treaty placed under him. This right was taken over by us, together with the rights of the clans, which included their right to the lands occupied by them, and which, in most cases, were the causes of their intertribal wars. It is therefore absurd to say that, when any of these chiefs seek our protection in consequence of injustice or oppression by the Pondos, that they are to be driven from their land.

The most extraordinary point, however, in the proceedings is, that the Pondos say they failed to see in what they were indebted to the Government for existence or prosperity. Quite the opposite sentiment has repeatedly been expressed to me in letters by Umqikela while I was Secretary for Native Affairs, and that these sentiments are not an empty compliment to Government can be abundantly proved by the past history of the Pondos.

On the dispersion of the tribes by Chaka in the beginning of the present century, the Pondos would have shared the fate of the Fingoes had it not been for the rugged country between the Lower Umzimvubu and Umtata, in which they concealed themselves from the Zulus, thus escaping extermination or final expulsion; and even here they owed their security only to the fact that they had been so stripped and spoiled of their cattle by the Zulus, that when, about 1830, they made their last expedition against the Pondos they obtained very little booty.

So impoverished had the Pondos become, that, at a muster of Zulu warriors in 1837, at the residence of Dingaan, I heard them ask for permission to make fresh conquests, begging to be permitted to go and destroy the children of Hintza and Gubencuka (i.e. Gcaleka and Tembus), who had many cattle, the Pondos being regarded as being already destroyed, and offering no inducement to an invading army in the shape of cattle. On the same occasion, at the muster of the (?) Impahlo Regiment, which had taken a leading part in the raids upon the Pondos, under their Colonel, Molanda, who then held the rank of General, they used a war song celebrating the conquest of the Pondos, from which I may quote the following translations of a stanza:—

> He (i.e. Dingaan) destroyed the cattle of Sigenu (Pondos);
> He destroyed the cattle of Isangwena,
> Who fled and sank in the Umzimvubu;
> Oh! take them by their heads and submerge them in the waters.

Do they not see the destroying bird is wrath—
He is raging;
He is the lightning of the earth.
The lion returns ;
The King of Zulus returns victorious.

This song, from which I have quoted, was in celebration of the last expedition of the Zulus against the Pondos, when they so concealed themselves that they were represented as sinking beneath the waters of the Umzimvubu. Their earliest missionary, who must have gone to Pondoland about 1830, describes them as being then so miserable and impoverished by the Zulus that they had not catttle sufficient to make skin coverings for themselves, but hung about their bodies coverings made from the Indian corn husks tied together.

Up to 1842 Faku himself lived in the rugged country on the Umgazi, while the majority of his people lived in the chaos of mountains extending from the lower Umzimvubu to the Umtata ; and one clan at least, namely that of Siyoyo, crossed the Umtata and became tributary to the Gcalekas. In 1840 the power of the Zulus was broken by the Emigrant Boers. Since then the Zulus have recovered their former position and power; but we now form an impassable barrier between them and the Pondos, otherwise, this unwarlike tribe, with their now large herds of cattle, would be as much at the mercy of the Zulus as they were in the days of Chaka and Dingana; and in all probability would have been long since driven out from the Umzimvubu, in whose waters the Zulu song represents them as hiding themselves.

Since our military expedition in 1842 passed up to Natal, the Pondos came out of their hiding places, and the pasturage being good in the country they were thus enabled to occupy, the few cattle that they had preserved from the Zulus multiplied and increased rapidly. To the ordinary increase of their stock they added by the cultivation of tobacco, which they sold to the tribes which had not been spoiled by the Zulus, for young cattle and goats. And Pondo tobacco became known and appreciated even to the borders of the Cape Colony, and the Pondos of the present day are thus the largest and wealthiest tribe between the Tugela and Fish River. This has been the result of British protection for only thirty-six years, though now ignored by the Pondos.

It is true that the Government has never given the Pondos active protection; this has never been necessary since they came under our control; nevertheless, they have been more benefited by our presence in Natal than if matters had been such as that they required active intervention. They have by us been entirely secured from external aggression, but have had internal feuds of their own making.

Umqikela has broken his treaty obligations, and now adds ingratitude to his offence, ignoring the benefits secured to the Pondos through us, and the obligations they are under to us in consequence. These benefits were ever frankly acknowledged by Faku. Umqikela and Damas have also admitted them. Umqikela charges the Government with having broken the Treaty of 1844 in the matter of Bell, who shot a Pondo. In this case there appears unfortunately to have been a miscarriage of justice. Bell was tried at Maritzburg for murder, and was acquitted in the ordinary course of law by the verdict of a jury. Government could do no more than they had done, neither have they failed in a single instance in faithfully observing every stipulation binding upon them.

The Government could not listen to the demand of Umqikela that fifty head of cattle should be paid to Umqikela for Bell's offence; they could deal with the culprit only according to law; neither had Umqikela, by virtue of the treaty or any other arrangement, any right to make the demand; and the question may be asked of him upon what principle the demand for fifty head of cattle was based, and if he had ever exacted the same number from any of his leading men and others for the many murders they commit on the charge of witchcraft, and of which Umqikela says he disapproves?

(Signed) C. BROWNLEE,
Resident Commissioner, Native Affairs,
Cape Colony.

HISTORY OF THE AMAXESIBE SINCE 1840, AS NARRATED BY THE PONDOS DURING A MEETING HELD AT NGOZI ON 27TH, 28TH & 29TH MAY 1880.

(Extracted from Original Minutes of Proceedings.)

Umqikela: Let the Government, I say, act friendly to me as I have to it. The Government must take away the Amaxesibe; their tricks and evil designs will bring me into trouble with Government. Do not think I was angry with you or the Government yesterday. Do not infer that from my remarks; but I am angry with the Xesibes through their occupying my ground. Let the Government listen to my wish about the land—my land—which the Amaxesibe occupy. These Amaxesibe will, I know, betray me to Government. Griffith told me that the Amaxesibe were my people, and Sir Henry Barkly said the same; and besides, they are my people by right of inheritance. At the meeting at Umfundisweni Griffith said to Jojo, "Jojo, you belong to Umqikela." Griffith then asked Makaula: "To whom does Jojo belong?" and Makaula said, "Jojo belonged to Faku. Through a girl Jojo and Faku quarrelled and separated. Jojo ran to Ncapayi and told Ncapayi "that he was being killed about a girl." Ncapayi said, "I must report this to Faku, because I am Faku's dog." Faku allowed Jojo to remain with Ncapayi because both Jojo and Ncapayi belonged to Faku. Faku said to Ncapayi, "Look after Jojo, he is my child. Jojo then sent an ox to Ncapayi, but Ncapayi would not accept it. Jojo insisted upon Ncapayi taking the ox; so Ncapayi then said, "If you insist upon my accepting an ox, give me that ox which you have called "Bodhl'ijike." Faku at this time was living at the Umgazi, Jojo at the Inyazi. Jojo did not remain a year with Ncapayi. He fell out with the Bacas and then came back to Faku.

Umqikela continued: Faku, as I have just said, was, at the time I am speaking of, living at the Umgazi. Jojo went back to Faku, and said, "Faku, father, the Bacas are killing me; take me back." "Faku said, I never told you to be running about in the mountains, so come back." He then told Jojo to go and live at the Umsikaba. Jojo did not remain long at the Umsikaba. He had a row with the Amambula, and left and went to live at the Emgodini. Faku was at this time living at the Umzimhlava. This was the year in which Damasi went to the other side of St. John's River, between the time of the wars of '35 and '46. After Ncapayi had "eaten up" the Amambula, Ncapayi said to Jojo, "Give me some of the oxen you have taken," so he gave him ten. Faku said, "Jojo, why do you do this? You are my man, and the Amambula my people." Jojo replied, "The Amambula abused me, that is why I ate them up." There were many cattle of Faku's and Bekameva's and Cingo's taken by the Amaxesibe; but Faku took no notice of the matter, and did not punish Jojo. The people wanted Faku to send an "impi" to punish Jojo, but Faku would not allow it. The Amambulu, a portion of the Imizizi, and some of the Amandela went out on the sly against the Amaxesibe and took thirty head of cattle. Faku left the Umzimhlava and came to the Emtsila· We then had peace. Faku did not want war. The Amaxesibe used to come and visit at the Great Place. I was then about the age of Josiah Jenkins (22 years). Two years after we came to the Emtsila Jojo left Emgodini and went to Inthlinzi and Swani to live. From the Swani they went to where they now are. Whilst Jojo was at the Emgodini he did not do anything wrong to Faku, if I except that just before leaving the Emgodini a man of Jojo's, by name Petella, was smelled out. He ran away to Bandezi. Patella had with him thirty head of cattle, calves included. After Patella had been at Bandezi's a little time he returned to his old home for the purpose of bringing away his family. Jojo had him caught and killed. Jojo left and went to Inthlinzi to live. Jojo demanded of Faku the cattle of the murdered man. Faku refused to give them up, and said that as this man Patella had taken refuge with him, and went back to get his family, "You ought not to have killed him. You know well our custom. When a man from me seeks refuge amongst your people he is safe. You know, Jojo, what I say is true." So this thing was apparently ended; but Jojo was not satisfied with what Faku did, but Jojo left off talking about the matter. Whilst Jojo was living at the Inthlinzi the Amaxesibe army went out against the Izilangwe, and took from them 300 head of cattle, and killed two influential men, Mahoki and Mayiweni. I was a youth at that time. After this they went out to fight against the Imizizi. Vang'indaba, the Chief Umditshwa's father, was slain, and five herds of cattle were taken by the Amaxesibe. Jojo had with him the Amajali. We heard the war-cry, and the Amantshangasi and others turned out. Two days after a man came from the Imizizi to report to us that Vang'indaba was dead, killed on his own kraal by the Amaxesibe. When Faku heard this he was greatly surprised at the conduct of the Amaxesibe, so I, Umqikela, said to Faku, "Let us go with an army against Jojo." So I collected an army at the Great Place. Faku came from Tansi's and found the army assembled, but he would not let us go, and the army dispersed by his orders. The Imizizi messengers were still at the Great Place when the army was sent away. Two months after the Imizizi came to Faku and said, "We must putuma, for our Chief is dead;" but Faku would not agree, and said to them, "You must not go out to fight against Jojo. I am crying as well as you for Vang'indaba." Faku sent and reported this to Sir Theophilus Shepstone (Somtseu). The messenger of Faku returned without any answer. I know what I am stating to be true. Nevertheless, and in spite of Faku's wish to the contrary, the Imizizi went out against the Amaxesibe. We did not accompany the Imizizi; only the Amajali went out with them. Of the Imizizi a great many were slain. The cattle were taken by the Amayalo. After this Jojo attacked Umyeki and Susungulu. Faku said, with reference to the attack made by the Imizizi and their defeat, "I told you not to go out; you acted contrary to my advice." After this Bolo, a Xesibe, came to Gwanya's, a man of Sontsela's, pretendedly on a visit, late at night. Gwanya took from him two assegais and a stick. Gwanya said to Bolo, "What makes you come here at this time of night? You are a spy." Bolo, on his road home, met a man driving three head of cattle. He took them from him and went home with them. The cattle were never restored. We sent back the assegais and stick, but the Amaxesibe would not receive them. Faku never took any steps in the matter, but let it stand. Some of the Amandela were coming from the Macis, driving six head of cattle. The Amaxesibe took the cattle from the Amandela, alleging that they did so on account of a fee ("Umnyobo") being due to them on account of a girl. Faku denied all knowledge of the matter, and even to this day we know nothing about the girl. After this Dlagana, a Xesibe, came to Umayabeni and stole from him twelve head of cattle. Umayabeni went out and stole in retaliation ten head of cattle from the Amaxesibe. This was the commencement of the stealing. Again, Umayabeni went out and stole fourteen head of cattle from the Amaxesibe.

Ndunge (a councillor): What we are now speaking of is only ("ingxakanxaka") of secondary importance. The Xesibes did these things although they were Faku's people. During Faku's lifetime we went out with our "impi" (army) whilst the Amaxesibe were living at Inthlinzi. We went out without Faku's knowledge or consent, because we were angry at the death of Vang'indaba. The lower division of the army was scattered and Bekameva taken prisoner. Twal'incolo was killed. He was with the upper division. This we did to punish them through their having killed Vang'indaba. This is all I have to say. The sun is burning me. Let the Government adhere to the boundary as defined by Griffith.

Fadana: All this has been said because the Chief has been giving out the Amaxesibe stock. All this is a disgrace, for Jojo is only a petty chief and a dog.

British Resident: I have been much interested in the history of the Amaxesibe which you have given me. It will be forwarded to Government.

The foregoing is a faithful transcript from the original minutes.

(Signed) J. OXLEY OXLAND,
British Resident, Eastern Pondoland.

June 17, 1880.

MINUTES OF CONFERENCE
BETWEEN J. M. ORPEN, BRITISH RESIDENT, AND THE XESIBE CHIEF, JOJO, ON THE 24TH & 25TH APRIL, 1874.

(Return relative to the Disturbance in Pondoland, 1880.)

Jojo said I am come to throw myself upon Government with my country, from which I was driven by Chaka, and to which I returned when he came to an end, and in which I have ever since lived. I then found my first enemy in it from the Pondo side. This has been ever since the death of my father Umjoli and my grandfather Usinama. I have grown up among that enemy. When we returned to our own country there were no old men among us: we were all young men, and none had the wisdom to think of reporting these circumstances to Government. After I was circumcised I was again attacked by Pondos, and then I reported myself to Mr. Shepstone. I was told to stay where I was and not give up my country. He said if I was attacked where I then was, I was to remove to Ibesi, but I refused. I said I did not see the rightfulness of it, or why I should leave my own country to go to that of other chiefs; but I was prepared to die in the country of my forefathers. I saw then, my enemies, coming and attacking me. Mr. Shepstone told me not to attack the Pondos, for I had once made an attack and killed a Pondo chief. After that I stood altogether on the defensive. Mr. Shepstone said he was sorry for me as I was so young, and thus fighting. I said therefore I should remove to some distance from the enemy to Umsintlanga. It was not because I was beaten or scattered, for whenever the Pondos attacked me I always repulsed them. Three Pondo chiefs, Faku's own relatives, have fallen in their attacks upon me. I am not going to count those on my side, for in each attack chiefs of Xesibes have fallen. Ten of Faku's chiefs, who are subordinate but not relatives, have fallen. I said to Mr. Shepstone I wished him to receive me with my country; but he said he was unable to do so, as he said the country belonged to Government. I said, Yes, it does belong to Government, for Government stood up for it when it was destroyed by Chaka. It did not belong to Faku, for Faku was assisted at the same time. The Pondos are no chiefs who can claim the country as theirs, so as to give them power over other chiefs. When has Faku the right to claim power to subordinate other chiefs; He is only given country by Government. Faku's only words were these, in attacking the Xesibes: "That he had a treaty with Government, showing the country belonged to him." This was his only plea. I said I shall never leave this country till Government, who allows us to live on food, finds us here. My having come here to-day is through the acts of the Pondos. After the meeting with Mr. Griffith, Umqikela then said to Mr. Griffith he would drive us out within seven days out of his country. On these words of seven days Mr. Griffith caused me and Adam Kok to leave the meeting, as he said it was coming to a fight. Mr. Griffith said each of us (Jojo and Kok) must leave some men to hear about the line, and we were to go home. When those men came from the meeting we heard nothing about the country. I looked forward to my former words, which I had spoken to Mr. Griffith about the original boundaries of the Xesibes at Umsikaba, pointing that with the country they occupied before Chaka's wars. My having come to-day is to tell you how far our country extended, for Mr. Shepstone was unable to receive me and our country first. And then Mr. Griffith, when I begged him, was still unable to do so. Our country extended in this direction to Umnceba, which is over the Umzimvubu. It includes Tabankulu. It reached Umsikaba, and down it and across to Umtamvuna River, and up it to the Ingeli Mountain, from which it flows. On the south it went as far as Lepongonepo. I am here to-day to bring forward the circumstances in which we are in that country of ours, for we are in course of being moved out of it. I am coming to report to my father that I am wondering to see an old chief, who has never left his own country to attack another chief, being deprived of his country. I wish to know from my father, the Government, what my fault is, for Government took that country from Chaka. I wonder that other chiefs, lately come into the country, are granted ground; while I, who was born in it, am given nothing. Lehana, Lebenya, Zibi and Kok have received grants, and I have received nothing, though born in the country belonging to me. I beg to be told the faults that I have committed. All the chiefs who have been requesting Government to receive them have been received, together with their country, as in the case of Faku. My father and grandfather were never subordinate to any chief. It was I who was the first one to be subordinate; that is, placing myself under Government. That country belonging to me I have brought it to the Government, for it did not belong to me but to Government, which has given shelter to all natives. Now it perceives my distress. Neither I nor my father or grandfather ever attacked the Pondos; and to-day, when I present myself to you, I have been restraining myself, fearing to commit myself with Government. I have only defended myself. But now, from the day Mr. Griffith left, the Pondos have been driving me out of my country. They come at me with their treaty with Government, and say it gives them authority to drive me out of my country. Before Griffith came they only attacked me; but since he came they have been continually taking possession of my country, saying the treaty gives them a right to it. They said that in public before Mr. Griffith. I put a question to the Pondos that day, asking, did not the treaty only give them their own country and not include other tribes? I asked, could it add anything to my country without my knowledge, for, at the time of the treaty, there was no chief of Xesibes subordinate to Pondos? To-day I have to state that, exactly in accordance with the words spoken to Mr. Griffith by the Pondos, they have been exactly what they said they would do. Now I come to you with a question: Since the Pondos never before flocked into my country and occupy it, I say they were influenced by their having made that statement so openly before Mr. Griffith. It is that which has given them, and now, to-day, they have surrounded me on all sides,

They have come in, as they said they would before Mr. Griffith' in order to drive me out of my country, or make me leave to go under Adam Kok; and, to-day, I have come to you to beg for existence, for I have restrained myself ever since I asked to be received under Government, and Mr. Griffith ordered me to remain quiet. And I am afraid now a collision will take place, for the Pondos are pressing close upon us and among us, and my young men may break out. I ask now the question: Whence have the Pondos received power? I have come to you to my home to ask that question, and why has my country been twice taken from me without my knowledge? for I consider Faku first stole my country without my knowledge by his treaty with Government, and now I consider it has been stolen a second time at Mr. Griffith's meeting for Kok, and I were told to leave, and while I was absent it was stolen by the Pondos. I beg now you will go and have my country pointed out to you—that I may have its old boundaries pointed to you—that you may be able to tell me plainly in my ears that you will not receive me. My coming here is in reality for this purpose. I wish our whole country to be under Government, and that the Pondos should go back to their country; that, when I go back to my village, I may have a pleasant sleep, knowing you have received me. I have come being afraid to break the order left with me that I was not to spill blood. I want that the old kraals of my father and grandfather, where they were born, should be received by Government. I wonder greatly at the act of Faku in taking possession of the country of other chiefs. My last words are these: Faku himself, when attacked. by Chaka, went to represent his case to Government, as I have done. If it please Government to receive me with my country, I would beg Government to send some officer to go with me to remove that school, which has been removed from its former place into the Xesibe country by the Pondos, in order to take possession of my country, with a thing which is begotten by Government that I could not attack, and they have used it in attacking me. I wish that the officer of Government may be appointed to live there at Macingo (Emfundesweni Mission) who may see to the acts of Jojo. The cause of my suffering is that the Pondos wish me to be under them, whereas I have said that I am under Government. They wished me under them that they may have power and numbers to press back Europeans. I refuse that. I refuse to go where I have been ill-treated, and because I cannot stand against Government, for Government is my true home. Faku may receive other chiefs who consider him stronger than Government. I don't. I wish my name enrolled among those who have been received by Government, like those of Umditshwa's and Umhlonhlo's, that I may save my own head. All these chiefs attacked by Umqikela are attacked in order to strengthen himself, because he wishes to be strong against Government. I do not wish Government's enemies to be strengthened. I hope to go back to my country with the good news that the Pondos are to go back to their own country, to Xura and Umgazi. In those three parts of my ancestors' kraals where I have lived cattle were never taken by the Pondos; they always got them away. Thus far I say and conclude. Jojo, asked the name of his father, grandfather, etc., says the line reaching backward to Xesibe is as follows:—Umjoli, Usinama, Mayaba, Gcuma, Mndiba, Gantuli, N'Tswaelana, Ndi, Umgam, Xesibe. All these were born and died in that country of ours. There are other separate Xesibe in Natal, and others, our relatives, over Umtata.

Asked to give the history of the tribe, beginning about Chaka's wars, Jojo and his councillors narrate the Xesibe were first attacked by the Amatumzela, under Cinza, who first caused some of them to retreat. After that Chaka's own army came, and he began to push us, Pondos and all, towards Bongone (the Frontier Kafirs?) to Umtata, and the Bashee. When we were at the Umtata, Chaka sent his great general, Umgotuba, with a message to all the conquered chiefs that they were to come to Chaka. Sinama, the Xesibe chief, sent his general and a subordinate, and Chaka said they were to tell Sinama to re-occupy his old kraals, he would not attack them again, and he gave a number of cattle and a blanket to Sinama. (The Pondos also sent in their submission, and Chaka was assassinated after receiving it in presence of their deputation, September 23, 1828). The Xesibes began to return in order to re-occupy their old kraals. But, when peace was established with Chaka, then we had to contend with the Pondos. The Xesibes never gave cattle to the Pondos as tribute in Sinama's time. Some cattle were given them for doctoring Sinama, when they asked him to join to help to defend each other against the Zooloos, but they never "Ingenad." The father of Ngqungushe, Nyauza, had a daughter married to Sinama, Jojo's grandfather. During the flight she took Jojo as a little child to Pondoland, while her husband was in flight with the tribe to Umtata. Sinama died there. The widow, Bangciswa, did not give cattle to Faku; but she offered him ivory, which he refused. She then left with the children, and went to the tribe towards Umtata to Mkwenkweni, and Faku immediately afterwards sent an army to attack the sons of Umjoli. Faku had sent a message to Ncapayi to ask him to help to destroy the line of Xesibes, lest they should become strong as in former times. The plot was agreed upon, and the attack made on both sides. The Pondos were beaten by the Xesibes, but the Bacas, meanwhile, were capturing cattle in the rear—a great number. The Xesibes then sent cattle to Ncapayi to ingena to him, and Ncapayi consented, and withdrew from his arrangements with Faku. The chief Umjoli was then dead, and the grown men had nearly all been killed, and it was only the widow and her mother who were taken to the Bacas. After this the Bacas(?) attacked Ncapayi (Faku?) at Izalo and Xura (Palmerton), and Umqikela's present residence. The Xesibe then separated from the Bacas, and returned to their own country. Jojo was then a boy. The great men left by Sinama accompanied Jojo and his grandmother, Bangciswa, to Umsikaba, where they were to settle on the frontier of their old country, the line between them and the Pondos. When they arrived there, Faku sent a message to

Bangciswa that she must send cattle. She consented and sent one cow; it was refused, as the ivory she formerly offered him had been, and Faku said he wanted 100 head. The great men of Sinama, who were with Jojo refused Jojo was then a young man, and he agreed with them and turned the cow into his kraal, and said this request will never be complied with. This is all we know about giving cattle—that cow which was refused. The next new thing was this : A chief of the Amambuli, Ngobo, came to the Xesibe. He was sick with his stomach blown up, and a Xesibe chief, named Sinama, cured him. He went away toward Pondoland, having cattle of Sinama's with him. Some were for a girl, and some were for doctor's fees. Jojo sent after him for those cattle. He was then circumcised. Ngobo said, in answer, how high can Jojo reach with his hand. I will not give up the cattle. Jojo collected his men, overtook Ngobo, and nearly finished his race. This was down on the Umsikaba, in the direction of the Pondos. A few days afterwards Faku turned out six armies and attacked the Xesibes. The Pondos were repulsed with considerable loss, and Faku went to report his defeat to Mr. Shepstone, and that the Xesibes had taken children of Ngobo's. Jojo heard this, and sent his brother Fikeni to Natal to hear what Faku had said, and say he was surprised by Faku's attack, as he had only been attacking his own subordinate, Ngobo. The Natal Government understood the matter well: that his subordinate was running away with some of his cattle, and its decision was in favour of Jojo, and that was the end of that affair. After this Jojo removed some of his kraals, as the Pondos were advancing to surround him. He removed a short distance to a place called Engodini, and spent five years there, after which, without being troubled there, he removed to Enhlenzi, below Macinga (where the Emfundisweni Mission has since been established). This is on the wagon road to Natal, where the meeting with Mr. Griffith was held. While Jojo was there there were wars of other tribes with which he had some connection! but we do not mention them as they did not concern Pondo affairs.

Nyeki, who had been subordinate to Usinyana in the neighbourhood of Sopongombo, asked Jojo to assist him; because the Imisire, a clan who are under the Pondos, had taken his goats; so Jojo went with him and attacked the Imisire by night, and Jojo's men killed their chief in the night. After Jojo and Nyeki returned, the Imisire followed them, and all of them who followed up were killed, so that matter ended. After that a year elapsed, and then the Pondos made a night attack on Jojo and Nyeki. Jojo killed them right off, as in the former case, and took Faku's son, Bekameva, prisoner. Swalingolo, Umqikela's brother, was killed. The taking of Bekameva prisoner was in accordance with advice of Mr. Shepstone's—advice to take prisoner and not kill chiefs. Faku went to report to Mr. Shepstone that his son was taken prisoner. Mr. Jenkins, his missionary, came, sent by Faku, begging Jojo not to kill him, and offering a hundred head of cattle, some of which he brought. All were not paid, for Bekameva went away in the night. That was the end of that matter. Jojo thought there would now be peace as he had prisoner Bekameva; but he only went away to collect an army and make war, which has continued till now, for as soon as he left a thief came and took Xesibe cattle. One of Jojo's went to do the same to the Pondos; but Jojo sent the cattle back, saying he did not like thieving, and if there must be war, let it be a fair open fight; but while Jojo thought now there is going to be peace Faku's army came out as at first. They did not succeed in capturing cattle again. They attacked him with a larger army six different times. It was after the second attack that Sir Walter Currie came, and immediately afterwards Emfundesweni was established, and the Pondo commando have since come through that station and rested there; but the Pondos were not able to occupy it till the Commission came. Before the seventh attack was made Adam Kok, on account of the professions of Umqikela, who had informed him that now there was peace between him and Jojo, asked Jojo to let the Pondos pass through freely. The road being thus opened for the Pondos, they were able to attack Jojo by surprise in a treacherous manner. In this attack a son of Faku's and a son of Jojo's were killed. The Pondos this time took a number of cattle, and Jojo could not recover them, being taken by surprise. Then the Commission came, and they told Jojo not to attack again, but to report to Mr. Shepstone; and Jojo asked to be placed under Government, and they desired Umqikela to keep peace. After the meeting sheep and goats of the Xesibe were taken and traced towards the kraals of Bekameva, and cattle were taken also. The spoors could not be followed, but a trader saw them going towards the Amacwera. Besides this, the Pondos at once, while the Commission was still in the country at Tsitsa, commenced pushing their kraals forward, and have continued doing so on to the Umtamvuna side to Ingeli and this side of the Insizwa, and we are squeezed up. They are now forcing their cattle between our kraals, and they say next year they will pick up our gardens, and they have already commenced interfering with them, and have compelled some of us to remove. We asked the Commission to ask Government to receive us, and it is on account of their instructions and our waiting for an answer that we have retreated and not resisted these encroachments and aggressions. They told us not to fight, but to report to Mr. Shepstone; and we reported and nothing has come of it.

After an adjournment, Jojo's councillors said, We have only to add this: that Ngqungqushe, Faku's father, made war upon the Amabomvana and was killed in that war. A large portion of the Pondos then refused to acknowledge his son Faku, and ran away to Sinama, who eat them up and drove them back to Faku, telling them to acknowledge him. This was related at the meeting with Mr. Griffith, and the Pondos acknowledged it. It proves that Faku was indebted to the Xesibe for their chieftainship, and that they were independent before Chaka's wars. The Pondos were not numerous. Many clans who, before that, were subordinate to the Xesibe, after those wars and the treaty Faku obtained from Government joined him on account of the treaty, and by such accessions he became powerful.

The Resident explained to Jojo that placing himself under Government would cause the Government to have judicial authority and appeal from him, and that witchcraft punishments would be prohibited, murders tried by Government, a census taken, hut tax imposed, etc., to all which Jojo assented (living on the border of Natal, he knows it all). The Resident then asked, was, he understood, Jojo's request to be conditional, or all the boundaries he had named being cleared by Government. After consultation, Jojo said, I wish to place myself, with my whole country, under Government, for the Pondos have not beaten me. The country is mine; it is also the Government's. It may be that Government, in receiving it, may not wish to keep all of it. The reason I retreated from parts of my country was that Mr. Shepstone advised me not to fight, and the reason that the Pondos have come in is that the Commission ordered me not to fight but report. The Pondos have not conquered it. I consider that Faku stole the country after my father died, and I was still a sucking boy. He could not do so while the men were alive, and I wonder at this act, seeing that Faku was nourished by the Xesibe. That, when I was destitute, he did not nourish me, but stole my country, though we were an independent tribe. I do not see how he could give the country to Government. I want to hear from Government how the country of one independent tribe could be given away by another, by whom it was not defeated. I should like to hear the Pondos prove that any chief of Xesibe was subordinate to them; if they cannot prove that, then they must admit that the Xesibe have a right to their country. To-day I resemble Faku when he gave himself up to Government, only that Faku did not give himself up to be taxed, and I do give myself up to be taxed as a subject. I wish to be begotten by Government. Government must teach me its rules, so that I may not dispute anything which Government directed me to do, that Government may receive us in that country which was never taken by any other tribe. I am wondering to see that our country was taken from us in a deceitful way through my being young. I wish to know whether Government has ceded our country to Faku by talking, whereas Faku was never able to take it by arms. In my grandfather's time, or my father's time, or yet in my time, they never were able to scatter me in that country. Is a child to be deprived of his patrimony because he is young? To whom has Umqikela's ground been given, the ground of his father, now he is dead? I allowed the Pondos to advance in consequence of Mr. Shepstone's mediation and the Commission's instructions, and to keep from war I had to keep shifting. This appears to me as if, when a man is told and tries to avoid war by keeping on shifting, he becomes a loser. I wish now to know from the father of both of us, of Faku and me, one father, the Government, if that is right, and is it its rule.

The Resident told Jojo he would report his words to Government, and communicate its answer to him.

CONDITIONS UNDER WHICH THE AMABACA CHIEF MAKAULA AND HIS PEOPLE BECAME BRITISH SUBJECTS.

(From Appendices of the Government Commission on Native Laws and Customs 1883.)

It appears that the chief Makaula made his first application to be taken over as a British subject in 1872, and in 1875 the Secretary for Native Affairs informed him that the Government was ready to accede to his oft-repeated request.

The following are extracts from the Minutes of a Meeting held at Kokstad on the 9th of October, 1875, before the Government Commissioners, Messrs. C. D. Griffith, S. A. Probart, and T. A. Cumming.

Present: The Baca Chief Makaula, with a number of his councillors and followers.

The President informed the chief Makaula that he had heard that he wished to see the Commission, and also that the Rev. Mr. White had shown him a letter from the Secretary for Native Affairs addressed to him (Makaula) dated Cape Town, 14th August 1875, No. 564.

The chief Makaula replied, his object in seeing the Commission was to say that he wished to be taken over by the Government; that this has been his wish ever since the Commission of 1872 was here. This is the first point. Secondly, that he wished to inform the Government that he has not yet been put fully in possession of the country, as defined by the said Commission of 1872, that there is a dispute as regards four different points in the said boundary lines.

The President further informed Makaula that he wished him to understand that when he became a subject of the Queen's Government every person, be he chief or common man, would be free to go to the Magistrate, with his complaint, without being compelled to go to the chief first. That the magistrate will be there to represent the Government, to whom, of course, the chief is a subordinate.

The President further remarked that when he last saw Makaula in 1872, he fully explained to him what was meant by becoming a subject under the Government.

To which Makaula replied that he recollected what was told him.

The President then informed Makaula that the chief points were—

1st,—That every person shall have the right of taking his suits or complaints to the magistrates without let or hindrance.

2nd,—That the people will have to pay taxes.

3rd,—That the Government will not allow any person to be put to death or beaten for witchcraft or any "smelling out" or eating up, etc., etc., etc.

The President then asked Makaula whether he wished the Government to take him and his people over on those conditions.

Makaula replied, "Yes, that is what I wish. I fully understand the conditions."

The President asked Makaula if there was anything further that he wished to state to the Commission in order that it might be forwarded to the Government.

Makaula replied that he wanted the Government to give him a magistrate for himself and his people, and to be taken over: and he wishes the Commission to mention to him before his headmen, who are here present, upon what conditions the country would be taken over, so that they might have an opportunity of replying.

The chief Makaula afterwards stated that in consideration of his giving up his position and power as chief, he wished to have an annual allowance made to him, and further stated that he wished to submit the names of the following chiefs and headmen to the notice of the Government, in order that he might get an annual allowance, namely:

Diko,	Sohlahla,
Dabula,	Maqubu,
Mabeleni,	Umleli,
Xamtwana,	Sixanto,
Umtemquan,	Gweva,

Tyntyn.

Makaula further stated that he and his people were quite of one mind about giving over the country, but he wished to ask the Commission whether it would be compulsory that any and all cases should be taken before the magistrate before being brought to him.

The President replied that of course no one would be prevented from going to his chief if he felt so inclined. That the people would be free to choose for themselves, whether to go to the chief or the magistrate in any little matters of dispute between themselves, but that in all criminal cases the magistrate was the proper authority to whom such cases must be taken.

HISTORICAL SKETCH OF THE PONDOMISE TRIBE AS TAKEN FROM "VETE," THE SON OF UMZIZIBA.

BY MR. F. P. GLADWIN.

(From Appendices to the Government Commission on Native Laws and Customs 1883.)

As far back as I have heard of our history, it dates back as far as the time when our ancestors lived at the Dedesi, which is near to where Langalibalele crossed the Quathlamba, at a river called the Dedesi. There were then six chiefs living there. The name of our chief was Malangana. The term Amampondomise was applied to us by the Halas. Four of the chiefs living at the Dedesi were Togu the ancestor of what are now called the Gcalekas, Hala the ancestor of what are now called the Abatembu, and Malangana and Rudulu, the fathers of the Amampondomise. The Amampondo separated from us before this time, and crossed the Umzimvubu (St. John's), lower down than we did.

The Amampondomise went to the sources of that river.

Malangana had one wife, he had no children when he came to the Umzimvubu. After he had been there some time a son was born, and he was called Njanye, he was an only child.

After the death of Malangana and during the time of Njanye, Togu and Hala emigrated still further south, but Njanye remained at the Umzimvubu.

Hala first settled at Bencuti, Shawbury, and Togu at Ncolora. As the people increased the girls of our houses were married to them (chiefs of other houses), and became mothers of the chiefs.

Our first three chiefs had no more than one wife. The first that married more than one wife was Ntose, he had three wives, and by them he had three sons, namely, Cwera, Mpinga, and Ncwini, and from these came three clans, which still bear their names.

Ntose died of sickness at the Rode; at his death Cwera was considered the great Chief. Ncwini married many wives and increased very much, and had kraals at the Umzimvubu, Kinira, Tina, Tsitsa, and Umtata, and died at Lotana.

Mpinga married wives and increased, but not so much as Ncwini.

At this time the Pondos were living beyond the Umzimvubu and were not many. These chiefs all died a natural death.

Ncwini died at Lotana having three sons, viz., Nxotwe, Dosini, and Cira. Cira the youngest chief became the most popular; he was the son of a Bushwoman, whom Ncwini made his wife. No dowry (Ikazi) was given for her, as the Bushmen did not demand it.

Cira then became chief and lived at Lotana near to Shawbury. He had one wife and had a son and only child by her, whose name was Umte. Cira died of natural causes, and was very young when he died, and was succeeded by his only son Umte, who also lived at the Lotana. There he married one wife and had four sons by her, namely, Sabe, who was the heir, Gqubusha, Rancolo, and Mhaga, and also died at Lotana.

Sabe became chief and married one wife, and had by her one son named Qeugebe. Sabe died at Lotana, leaving his son Qeugebe to succeed him, and he also died at the Lotana.

When Majola the heir succeeded his father Qeugebe he removed to the Umzimzubu to live at the kraals of his forefathers, there he died, and was buried in the river Umzimvubu, and is one of the five chiefs who were buried in water. Before the death of Qeugebe he had one son named Ngwanya who removed to the Tina, died there, and was buried in that river, leaving his son Pahlo to succeed him, who also died and was buried in the Tina, leaving his son Sontlo to the Chieftainship, who also died and was buried in the same way as his father and predecessors.

Mgabisa, who was second son to Pahlo, succeeded him and took charge of the children. When Mgcambi was a young man, Mgabisa, his guardian, took his cattle and removed to his side of the Tsitsa (where Mabasa now is) and had a great many people, as he had been the ruler.

Mgcambi remained at Qangqu and began a war; every army that he sent out against Mgabisa was defeated, and people were killed. Resho, a relative of the chief, begged peace for him. After this defeat four men were sent by night, and they went secretly to Mgabisa's hut, stabbed him with their assegais and took back Mgcambi's cattle. He then became ruler and died very young.

The Amangxabane clan fought among themselves, and they were at that time living at Ngwenyama. Bodi the elder was defeated, and sought help from the chief Mgcambi, who went out against the younger with Ncokazi and defeated him. He escaped to the Halas.

The chief Mgcambi was killed by the Amangxabane under Mcokazi, by an assegai wound during the fight, and was buried at Ncambela.

The Amangxabane were confiscated (sic) by the chief Valelo, a young brother who took charge of the late chief's families. He reared Umyeki, the heir apparent, he obtained the wives, three wives for him and then Valelo confiscated (sic) Umyeki, because as he alleged he had killed his father Mgalisa, and was told to go to Pondoland to Faku, whose mother was one of Umyeki's ancestors.

The tribe refused to allow him to go, fought with Valelo, and drove him off to Pondoland. He was then attacked by the Mfecane, driven off and killed by Notyantsu at the Nqadu. Then Diko his son went to Pondoland.

THE WARS.

The Amantuzela came from Natal to fight, but were defeated with great slaughter. Then Makinane came, and afterwards the Amabaca came with their families and stock and attacked us. We fought against them. They found the tribe severed by the internecine war of Valelo and Umyeki, and therefore weak, they drove us before them. The first battle was at Bencuti; we fought with them some days; they were encamped there and continued to attack until the third day, when we retreated and crossed the Tsitsa at many drifts, one party of our army, the Amangxabane clan, crossed near the waterfall, and the other sections at drifts higher up, for since they had crossed a freshet came down and they crossed with difficulty. Two men of the Amagqulusha were drowned. We then retreated to Umdumbo, the Bacas followed us, and encamped near us at the Nqadu Forests. I was sent with four others to Gubencuka chief of the Ama-Hala, they had previously been assisted by Ngcambi. * * * Now we went to give a War Cry to the Halas. Gubencuka collected his army for three days; he and his army went out and crossed at the Entshaba drift. The Pondomise came up and met them near Mbedashes tree, and made a combined attack on the Bacas. The main body was repulsed by Ngubencuka, but the Pondomise, Amagcina, and the Amaqwati were driven back. This partial defeat was not immediately followed up, and the Bacas went on to the Elukalweni-twenyanga, and there attacked the Halas, killed some of them, and encamped at the Gqutyini. This was winter time. In spring another combined attack was made on them by the Pondomise, Halas, Amagcina, and Gcalekas. The Bacas were surrounded, and by daylight the attack commenced, and they could not make much resistance, and were massacred and scattered, their cattle were seized, and their wives and children were made captives of war. They then escaped into Pondoland and served Faku. Their chiefs Madikana, Matomela, Mqukubeni and Vatshile, mother of Madikana, were killed, she, because it was supposed she had encouraged the Bacas in the war. We (the Pondomise) were then attacked by a Baca chief Golizulu (seen by women). He came from the north, and we killed him near Mount Belle. He came from the north to attack Umyeki, who was at that time living near Cumgce. The Pondomise turned out nine clans of the great house and Amangxabane, the second division Amagqubusha and the Ama-rudulu. The Bacas were repulsed, retreated, and were followed up from Bele to Tsitsa, and were routed, and those who remained escaped into the forest near the residency (Tsolo); we took all their cattle and some of their wives were captured, and to this day their offspring is amongst us.

Nonzaba, another Baca chief from the north, was going to attack us. He was seen by some people who had gone to hunt, at that time Valelo was living at the Umhlakulo, so Nonzaba and his army made for them and ate (i.e., captured stock); Valelo who had sore eyes at the time, went into some indonga to conceal himself, but a Pondomise woman told where he was concealed and the Bacas killed him. (The Pondomise were at this time in two divisions). We were living at (?) and heard the war-cry. The Amavelelo followed the Bacas towards the Embuto flats. We had there turned out and cut off their retreat, they came on and we attacked them from the front and Valelo from behind. They were all killed but three men. They had left their families and stock and had come out on a marauding expedition.

Then Tshaka came. He came to the Pondos first and plundered their cattle and drove them to the Umgazi. Faku sent the war-cry to Umyeki who was at the Umdumbi, and he was asked to send the war-cry to Gubencuka, he sent Sotuka and the son of Qilikwana, with word to the English and to the Gcalekas. The English and the Gcalekas came, but when they arrived they found that Tshaka had gone home, but that another tribe under Matiwana had come from the north and passed down the Xabane and Kalani, and had dispersed the Ama-qwati and eaten their cattle. They did not fight the English when they heard the reports of the guns. The Amangwana women (the tribe under Matiwana) shouted "Yinjaleya, Vajokeni noho val wa Ngezulu." (They are but dogs, drive them though they fight by thunder); they thought the report of the guns was thunder. The English army marched by night and attacked by daylight. The Amangwana made no stand, but fled and went into the bushes. The reports of the guns were very dreadful, none of the native allies fought, they just looked on in astonishment. The report of the cannon was fearful, it was directed into the bush; women and children screamed, and cattle bellowed, and all came out of the forest towards where the army was, and were captured (sic) that time four elephant tusks to the English, and they accompanied him to his country over the Umgazi, and the station of Palmerton was formed under Mr. Shepstone. Diko and Ncapayi went under Faku, and Faku said I want to get cattle, so he sent out his army first to the Amangxabane and plundered them, then to Umyeki, next he attacked the Halas, and sent them to the Hewu under the Umtivana (the chief). They (the Pondos) were the people that scattered the country, the Mfecane did not do much. They also ate up the Gcalekas. Then there were Faku, Diko, and Ncapayi.

The Pondomise under Umyeki then went to the Rode; they removed because they were in danger of being eaten. We repulsed Faku's army, and they could eat our cattle.

They became Mfecane Marauders, and we left them through that. After we left we heard that Faku and Ncapayi had quarrelled about a Baca who had done wrong and ran away to Faku, who would not give him up. They fought and Faku got help from the English to awe Ncapayi.

Umyeki died near the Cacadu. He was the first Pondomise chief that died out of their country. He was succeeded by Matiwana his son, so called after the Amangwana chief who was killed by the English.

All the tribes that were driven returned about the year 1846. When we got to the Hewu the Amaquati ate the cattle of the Ama-Nxintsa for some horses that had been stolen from the Gcalekas and concealed by a Quati with us, he was caught and eaten up, and in retaliation for this he ate up the ama-Nxintsa, and so they ate up the Amaqwati.

Mandela and Umditshwa were then living at the Cumgce and had removed from Faku. They then sent word to Matiwana that they heard that Fubu the Amaqwati chief was going to remove to the Orange River and they proposed an attack upon him. Tshulu and

Nzanya brought the message. Matiwana consented and began to take cattle from the Amaqwati. They turned out and the Amadiko came on behind. The Amaqwati followed up and out-flanked them. They got a commanding position, and as we advanced up they came down on us, and had the advantage in throwing their assegais, and we were compelled to retreat. Matiwana with part of the army was driving the cattle which had been captured, the Amaqwati attacked him, and killed many of them, and he, Matiwana, ran into a small bush and was followed by two of the Amaqwati, who took his assegais from him but did not kill him, as he was nephew to them.

The Amadiko came up and said if you are afraid of him move off we will kill him, we are accustomed to kill each other, and they stabbed him. They took his assegais and shouted to us saying, " Where is your chief?" After a while we sent people to seek for him, they found him dead with his chest ripped up, and part of the breast bone gone, and some umsenge wood was stuffed in the wound (sic). They went back to our kraals and took our cattle, excepting those belonging to the chief. We went back to the Cacadu to Umyeki, who was still alive. He wanted to eat us up because he said the tribe had left him to follow Matiwana, and that he had taken his cattle.

Umbali the uncle of Umhlonhlo became regent, and he left with the tribe. They came past the Umga, across the Inxu and Tsitsa to the Tina, and he went to Faku and reported his arrival. Faku said he could not rear another chief's child, and that Umbali was to go and live at the Tina with Mr. Hulley. Joyi came down to live with Umbali, and Jumba lived at the Tsitsa and along the Inxu. Joyi lived at the Nxakolo, and removed from there to Malepelepe, and from there to the Baziya, and Joyi reared Ngangelizwe, and when he became circumcised Joyi died. At this time Mabasa was regent for Umdit-shwa's tribe.

A BRIEF HISTORY OF THE PONDOMISE TRIBE,

AS ALSO A SHORT ACCOUNT OF THEIR LAWS AND CUSTOMS AS RELATED BY MABASA, LATE REGENT OF UMDITSHWA'S SECTION OF THE PONDOMISE, AND NOMALA, AN OLD COUNCILLOR, AND

Written by E. S. BAM, Interpreter to the Resident Magistrate, Tsolo, Griqualand East, and forwarded to the Commission by A. R. WELSH, Esq.

(From Appendices of the Government Commission on Native Law and Customs, 1883.)

The Pondomise originally lived at the sources of the Umzimvubu called the Dedesi. This is called "Eluhlangeni," which means a large lake, whence the Pondomise came out and inhabited the Umzimvubu.

When they increased they extended their habitations from the Umzimvubu to the Umtata River.

Their Genealogy is as follows:—

SIKOMO, who is the first chief known.

Njanye, son of Sikomo, who is father of
Malangana, who is father of
Ntose, who is father of
Ncwini, who is father of
Cira, who is father of
Saba, who is father of
Umhe, who is father of
Qengebe, who is father of
Majola, who is father of
Ngwanya, who is father of
Pahlo.

From Pahlo the Pondomise tribe split into two sections. Pahlo had five wives, and by them had four sons and one daughter, viz., Mamani, his daughter by the chief wife, and she therefore became head of the tribe, which is always thought a great pity to have a female (heir) heiress.

By the house of the direct line he had two sons, viz., Sigxum and Mgabisa respectively. This house is called Iqadi, which literally means that in case the chief wife bears no sons, a son of that house becomes the heir and head of the whole tribe. By the house of his youth he had one son called Mbingwa. This house is called Umsoko, and cannot succeed to the throne unless no other male is born to the chief, simply because he marries that house shortly after he has undergone the rite and ceremony of circumcision.

By the right hand house, Ukunene, Pahlo had one son named Sontlo and he died a natural death.

It so happened that after Pahlo's death Nyawuza, a Pondo chief, sent his daughter Ntsibaba to Mamani (Pahlo's daughter) although he knew that she also was a female. Thereupon Mamani chose her brother of the right hand house as bridegroom of her Pondo bride, thereby appointing Sontlo to be successor to her deceased father, leaving Sigxum, her brother by the Iqadi, who ought to have succeeded in her stead since she was a female.

Sontlo died shortly after, leaving no heir. But before he died he appointed Mgabisa, the second son of his father's Iqadi, to the chieftainship. After a time it was ascertained that one of Sontlo's wives was pregnant when he died, and she bore a son named Mngcambi.

Mgabisa and his elder brothers called upon Sontlo's wives to choose from among them those who would be their husbands instead of their deceased brother Sontlo. Thereupon the wives of the deceased made a large quantity of beer, and when it was ready the chiefs were called together, as also the chief's widows, and the chief widow chose Mgabisa as her husband, thereby confirming the appointment made by her husband at his death. Accordingly Mgabisa ruled the tribe until Mngcambi was circumcised, and he was appointed chief in the place of his father Sontlo, who died before he was born.

Mgabisa left the Umzimvubu with a·portion of the Pondomise who chose to follow him, and occupied the Tsitsa near where Mabusa lived in the Tsolo District previous to the late rebellion.

He had five sons by different wives, but we will content ourselves by inserting the name of his principal and chief son, namely Velelo.

While Velelo was still a youngster Mngcambi sent an army against Mgabisa, who defeated it with great loss and capture of cattle. He (Mngcambi) again sent another army, and it was also defeated.

Mngcambi then sent bribed men to Mgabisa's kraal at the Tsitsa, and they succeeded in assassinating him. Velelo and the other boys (his brothers) went with their father's cattle and widows back to the Umzimvubu and surrendered themselves to Mngcambi their cousin.

It must here be observed that Mngcambi and Velelo had one mother and two different fathers. Mngcambi brought up Velelo his half brother. After he was circumcised and became a young man a quarrel arose between Bodi and Ncokazi, both sons of Ribela, a Pondomise petty chief who occupied the country lying on both sides of the Umtata river.

Mngcambi collected an army to punish Ncokazi, the younger brother of the two, and he (Mngcambi) was wounded in the battle field and carried home a dying man, leaving Myeki as his heir, a little boy at the time.

Then Velelo became chief of both sections of the Pondomise tribe until Myeki was circumcised and married wives. Velelo then desired to appoint Myeki the lawful chief, but he declined, saying he was yet too young to govern the tribe.

It so happened that Myeki employed a doctor named Gotolo to make him a strong chief. When Velelo heard of this he sent and had Gotolo killed and his cattle taken.

Thereupon Myeki fled with his cattle towards the Umzimvubu river. Velelo sent his messengers to call him, but he refused to return, and ran into a bush, and from thence went to the Tina and took refuge among the Amatyam and Amanxasana, who occupied that tract of country. The Amatyam sent to Velelo for an explanation, and to demand Myeki's cattle, which Velelo refused to deliver, but said he wanted Myeki to speak to him. Thereupon Myeki sent an army to rescue his cattle, but it was totally defeated.

Here the Pondomise got broken up and were dispersed by different Zulu invaders, who expelled them to the Gungululu (Tsolo District) and the Umgazi now in Pondoland, as also the Xuka in the Engcobo District, and the Rode or Cacadu now in the St. Mark's District.

Myeki had many sons, his heir being Matiwana.

Velelo also had many sons of whom Diko was the heir. Mabasa, Velelo's second son, became Regent after Diko's death.

Velelo was killed in this District at the Gungululu by a Zulu chief named Nondzaba, who was also killed by the Pondomise near a kopjie within sight of the Residency here, hence its name—Nondzaba.

Diko had also a number of sons who are still surviving, of whom Umditshwa was his chief son and heir. Diko died a natural death at the Cumngce in Pondoland, and his brother Mabasa became Regent until his nephew Umditshwa became of age, to whom he resigned the Government of this section of the Pondomise.

In consequence of the late rebellion Umditshwa is a prisoner in gaol at Cape Town under a sentence of three years' imprisonment. He also has a number of sons, but the heir Mtshazi, by Kreli's daughter Nogqili, is as yet a little boy of about thirteen years of age. Thus far we have traced this section of the Pondomise, and will now trace the other section from Myeki's time up to the present time.

Myeki died a natural death at the Cacadu, leaving Matiwana as his heir.

When Matiwana was living at the Xuka a missionary of the name of Gladwin called upon Matiwana and suggested the removal of Matiwana to this territory, It was at the time entirely unoccupied. He agreed, and on his way was attacked and killed by Fubu (Dalasile's father) near the Baziya.

His brother Mbali (who is now living in Pondoland) became Regent, and he led the Pondomise (then only forty in number) and inhabited the Tina near the old road which is now one of the present boundaries between Qumbu District and Pondoland West.

When Mhlonhlo was circumcised Mbali refused to give up the chieftainship to him, saying Mhlonhlo was a son by the minor house. But Umditshwa said that it was right that Mhlonhlo should succeed his father, Matiwana, since he was a son by the house of the direct line— that is the Iqadi.

It is needless for us to mention his government of his people, his warlike nature and treachery in killing the gallant officer Mr. Hamilton Hope and his companions.

Umhlonhlo had in all eleven wives, two of them died years ago, and he had a number of boys, but his chief wife, also a daughter of Kreli's, died shortly before the rebellion, leaving only three daughters.

Umhlonhlo is now at large, having forfeited his chieftainship, his country, and people.

It may here be remarked that Majola, who appears as one of the chiefs mentioned in our genealogy, died a natural death near the Tina River, and his body was interred in a large pool of water in that river. In cases of drought Mhlonhlo and his predecessor Mbali used to kill an ox or oxen and the carcases of the animals were taken and thrown in the pool wherein Majola's body was interred, thereby supplicating for rain.

It is said that from Sikomo, Njanye, and Malangana, the Pondomise and the Amaxosa (Kafirs proper) were considered as of one race and origin.

The Pondomise had no fixed laws, but each succeeding chief laid down certain rules which he thought would fit his government of the tribe.

Their customs as practised by them were and are still of the following nature, viz.:—Circumcision, "Ukwaluka;" Girls undergoing the rite of Puberty, "Intonjane;" Marriage, "Ukwenda;" War Dances, "Umguyo;" Dances for Pleasure, "Imijadu."

When a number of boys are to be circumcised they are generally collected at one kraal where a beast is killed for them, and the meat of this beast no females are allowed to partake of, except young girls of four years or less. They then leave the kraal and go to an appointed place at the nearest river, where the boys wash their bodies and are then circumcised at sunset. A hut and a kraal are built for them at a distance, and they milk the cattle that are brought from the different parents of these boys, and the milk of these cattle no female is allowed to partake of. Two or three young men are chosen to take care of these boys. These are called "Amakankata." The boys remain at their kraal painted with white clay all over their bodies for a period of three or four months, and when they are perfectly healed, notice is given that a large quantity of beer is to be made. When it is ready a large number of oxen are driven to their kraal, and their hut and kraal are put in flames, and the boys rush with all their speed to the nearest and appointed drift of a river, where they plunge in and wash themselves in it. This being done they go home to a kraal fixed for them, then karosses prepared from the hides of cattle, or blankets now-a-days are given to each of them, and then they are warned to keep out of mischief.

They remain in a selected hut with the four or five young men who took care of them while they underwent circumcision. The men and women then drink the beer. They remain at that kraal for a few days and then disperse to their respective homes. When at their homes each of them goes among his friends, and a beast, goat or sheep, or assegai is given him by his relatives. This is called "Ukusoka."

The "Intonjane" (rite of undergoing the age of Puberty) is a custom that has also been in existence from time immemorial. When any woman reaches this age a hut is selected and a partition of mats made, behind which this girl lies or sits concealed. A number of girls and women "Amadikazi" (a number of women who have been married and have fallen out with their husbands or widows) are collected to take care of the said girl, but she is specially committed to the care of her immediate relatives, who cook her food as also that of the girls thus collected. The girls then dance a sort of dance called "Umngqu-ngqo," and the father and near relatives kill as many stock as their circumstances admit of. Then comes the "Umngqungqo" of women of the neighbouring kraals, which generally lasts for two days, and stock is killed for them either in cattle, sheep or goats as the case might be.

Numbers of young men and boys gather from different localities to this "Intonjane," and a sort of dance called "Umtshotsho," is always to be heard in this hut between the girls and the young men.

Here, in accordance with the Pondomise custom, the girls and the Amadikazi have the right of choosing their paramours or sweet-hearts. But in accordance with Amaxosa (Kafir proper), custom, young men and boys are not allowed to attend, and the old men choose one of them whom they call "Indindala" (a sentry) to choose from the girls paramours or sweet-hearts for the old men thus collected, and he has a right of punishing both men and girls who may break the rules laid down for that practice. It is called "Isiko" by the Amaxosa.

After a month or two perhaps the parents of this girl find that their food is diminished, and they then give notice that it should stop, or the "Intonjane" must go out as it is called. When that day comes, people from neighbouring localities come with numbers of oxen to honour the ceremony.

This is called "ukugqusha," the different oxen that come to the "Inkundhla" (middle of the kraal) are generally an ox or two by one young man one after the other. When that "Ibandhla" (company) has finished, their oxen are collected together and a mutual dance is performed. This is called "Inkondhlo." Then comes the grand dance of different companies under different headmen and minor chiefs. This is called "Amagwifa."

Sometimes eight or nine head of cattle are killed in honour of this ceremony (Intonjane) and the meat distributed among the different companies (Amabandhla) both of men and women, and the dance is finished.

Two or three days after this all the girls who had been the attendants of this "Intonjane" go to a forest and get firewood, which they take to the hut belonging to the mother or guardian of this girl as the case might be, and then disperse to their respective homes.

There are different modes of performing the rite of marriage which is called "Ukuzeka" or "Ukwenda." When a chief's daughter is intended to marry a chief, messengers are generally sent to the intended bridegroom with an assegai which is a token of the intentions of the father of the bride, and when the young man or his father gives his consent the messengers return to the father of such a girl and report such consent to him, and the father (if he be a chief also) calls a number of girls and women without consulting his daughter in any way. Then a beast is killed in honour of her departure, and when that has been consumed, the party sets off for the kraal of the young man, driving four or five head of cattle, and when they arrive at the kraal one of the cattle is killed and the remainder are left as the "Ubulunga" cattle, from which cattle she generally plucks hair from the brush, and she wears that as a charm against all misfortunes that may happen to her person. When the day comes for the tribe to see their chief's new wife, the bride and maids paint themselves red with red clay and then go out to the middle of the kraal, where they kneel for a short time and rise again to go to their hut. Then comes the wedding day, and sometimes innumerable numbers of people assemble, and dancing goes on. Numbers of cattle are killed; from six to ten head on this occasion.

For the woman who is to be the chief wife of a chief all the councillors, principal men, and others are called upon to give cattle towards the dowry to be paid for her, which varies from fifty to one hundred head of cattle, in accordance with the position she holds in her father's family.

One mode is for the lover of any woman, except a chief's daughter, to call a number of young men who go and carry the girl away either in the field or at her kraal to his home. As soon as they get there a sheep or goat is killed for the carriers, who are bound to watch this woman day and night till her friends come to demand dowry. When they do come, another beast, sheep or goat, as the case may be, is killed, and they eat that with her which is a token that from hereafter she remains as a wife to that husband, and *must* partake of their milk, because a woman never drinks the milk of her husband's kraal unless some animal is killed for the purpose.

There is sometimes danger in carrying away a girl by force, because her friends and neighbours sometimes turn out armed with assegais and kerries, and a fight follows. This is generally remedied by the carriers giving an assegai or by consulting the father of the girl previous to carrying her off.

The "Umguyo" (War Dance) is one of the principal customs among the Pondomise and the neighbouring tribes. When a chief thinks it proper he sends to his people and appoints a day in which they are to come to this "Umguyo," and they are bound to come armed.

When that day comes all those who are able to attend go to the chief's kraal armed with guns, assegais, and shields made of oxhide. The doctor, who is always also called, prepares his charms and doctors the men, making them brave and lucky from getting wounded. Sometimes hot water is boiled and some herbs put into it, with which to sprinkle the men; they sometimes or some of them get scorched. Sometimes black ants are scattered over their bodies, and although they bite very sore, if the doctor discovers anyone shaking them will give the parties thus discovered an assegai.

There are generally three celebrated seasons for this "Umguyo," viz.: beginning of spring, approach of new crops or green mealies, and when a chief is about to send his army against another chief,

The "Unyadu" (Dance for pleasure) is one where young men and girls of one locality invite their neighbours to an appointed kraal where they dance nearly all day.

The following rules have also been always in existence among the Pondomise and other natives, viz.: That a grown up male of any kraal, either son or father, has to pay a ransom called "Isizi" if any male dies from natural causes, either if it be the father or the chief son or heir dies. Formerly this ransom amounted to from five to ten head of cattle, but lately it has been reduced even to two head of cattle.

When the subjects of one chief quarrel and fight a general fine is inflicted upon the parties who may have fought, without any enquiry being made to find out the guilty side. This fine is called "Umhlanga," and the whole of it goes to the chief.

When a spoor of one or more animals is traced to a certain locality the inhabitants of such locality are called to it, and if they cannot trace it past that locality or to any kraal, the whole of the locality is held responsible, and a fine is imposed.

When such fine is paid, the owner of the missing stock is compensated, and the rest of the fine goes to the chief's place, or Great Place, as it is generally called among us.

Witchcraft is one of the most abominable crimes that the Pondomise practice. There are some people who are called "Izanuse" (Witchdoctors) and are dreaded by chiefs even for the power of their charms. When a witch doctor accuses any person of causing the illness of any individual, the accused party is tormented in many ways, perhaps by binding his hands and feet with fine cords, perhaps by scorching him with fire, and perhaps by first throwing water over the party and then shaking swarms of black ants over the body, which they bite in a most agonising manner. The accused is generally killed.

If he is killed by the common people or minor chiefs, the fine for his murder is ten head of cattle.

But when one is accused of witchcraft by causing the sickness of a chief, that party is killed and all his stock taken from him, and his family left to starve, and even driven out of the country.

If a chief's daughter is seduced by any person, the people of his clan forfeit their stock, and it goes to the Great Place.

Adultery was rarely practised by the Pondomise until they became mixed with the Kafirs proper. When any man was caught, confiscation of his stock followed, but if he committed that act with a chief's wife, death as well as confiscation of his property ensued.

The law of inheritance has also been in existence for many years. If a man marries one wife, and she bears sons and daughters, the first born becomes heir of his father's property, and all his sisters and brothers become his subordinates.

If he marries two wives, the son by the chief wife is only entitled to that portion of stock due to his mother's house, the son by the second house called "Ukunene" (right hand house) is entitled to all the stock due to his mother's house; but if he marries more than two wives, the off-spring of the two minor houses are subordinate to the two head houses; these houses are called "Amaqadi."

As to land tenure, all people are entitled to garden ground, but the right of land is solely in the power of the chief, and he allots garden ground in such a way as suits his convenience to dispose of the land. The chief has the power and right of appointing any person he may deem fit to the duties of alloting garden ground, but if any one individual is dissatisfied with any arrangement made by such appointed person, he has the right of appealing to the chief, whose decision is final. Any person removing from one locality to another has no right of disposing of his garden ground and kraal, but they again become the property of the chief, and any person who may be desirous of having them is bound to apply to the chief for them. The chief only has the power of allowing any person to remain in his country, as also of expelling anyone at his own disposal.

Bushmen are believed to have the power of bringing rain from the heavens, and cattle are often sent to them as an application for rain. They also have the right of collecting a small share of the crops after harvest is over, which is a thanksgiving for the rain they bring from the heavens, which enables the people to reap plenty of grain.

GENERAL HISTORY OF THE GRIQUAS.

(Report of a Commission to enquire into the causes of the outbreak in Griqualand East, 1879.)

The Griquas first became a settled people in 1813, when they located themselves at Klaarwater, afterwards called Griquatown. In 1800 they were wandering savages, living by plunder and the chase, with painted bodies, greasy powdered heads, and a filthy kaross for their sole covering. The only article of European clothing amongst them, until it came into vogue at the time of their settlement, was a rag in the possession of a female. Abandoned to witchcraft, drunkenness, and licentiousness, the plunder and murder of each other were common. They even plotted to take the lives of the missionaries, who for five years accompanied their wanderings. At the time of their settlement the people, being about 3,400 Griquas and Korannas in equal parts, counted four-and-twenty second-hand wagons amongst their possessions, while many had acquired a knowledge of masonry and wagon-making. They were in 1819 sufficiently advanced to attend the Beaufort Fair, doing business to the tune of 27,000 rix-dollars; repeating the visit next year with a drove of 700 cattle, and oxen drawing 27 wagons, laden with tusks, salt, skins, wheat and honey. The seizure of this party is said to have been ordered by Lord Charles Somerset, who was greatly incensed with the Griquas for refusing, some five years before, to furnish a contingent for the Cape Corps. They were in 1825 visited by traders, with clothing, gunpowder, firearms and brandy; and somewhere about this time a section of the people moved southwards to the country of Philipolis. The following was the position of the respective chiefs in 1822:—At Daniel's Kuil, Barends, who subsequently went farther north to Bootschap; Waterboer, at Griquatown; Cornelius Kok, at Campbell; and Adam Kok, sen., between the Vaal and Reit Rivers. These chiefs who were called Kaptyns, were assisted in the government by councillors selected from the chief men. The first treaty between a Native chief and Colonial Governor was made in 1834, Sir Lowry Cole and Waterboer being the high contracting parties. A similar engagement was afterwards entered into with Adam Kok, who was ratified in his ownership of the Philipolis territory. Kok's death was followed by civil war, Adam and Abram becoming rival competitors; but the former triumphed, and partially healed a tribal breach by marrying the widow of an elder brother. . . . . Owing to the unpopularity of an agent of the Colonial Government, a party now seceded from Griquatown, and, with some Korannas and others, went into the mountains, and hence assumed the name of Bergenaars. They were also called Bushmen, and dealt largely with Colonial traders for whose brandy and gunpowder they bartered slaves and cattle obtained in raids amongst Basutos and Bechuanas. With the extension of Colonial boundaries to the Orange River, the Bergenaars were removed beyond it, and the settlement then made was the real beginning of the town of Philipolis. Invited by Kok to join him, they refused, but afterwards sent him a petition to come to their help against the Kafirs. He came on the 20th June, 1826, and thus originated his connection with that township. Quarrelling with him in a few months, the Bushmen returned to their old haunts near the Vaal, the gap made by their defection being soon filled up with Namaquas and people from the Colony. Successful in an attack on Griquatown in 1827, but repulsed in a renewal of it, the Bergenaars turned a threatening front towards Matibi, the chief of the Batlapi's, who therefore deserted Kuruman for the protection of Waterboer, with whom they settled. Out of one difficulty into another. As the Bergenaars retired, the Boers advanced. The first Boer to settle north of the Orange River was Ockert Schalkwyk, who obtained a Griqua permit in 1828. He was alone, having left his family in the Colony; whence he was soon followed by others, and by a still larger number from Natal after their defeat there. Indeed, they began to look upon the land as their home. Trouble grew apace, and the helpless Griquas appealed under treaty to the British Government. Troops arriving, the Boers were checked, and Philipolis for a time preserved to its owners. Military aid was again invoked in 1845, when, on defeat of the Boers Sir P. Maitland and Mr. Porter proceeded to Philipolis, and blamed Kok for allowing the Dutch to get "a sort of legal footing in the country, where they were rapidly becoming too strong for him." At the battle of Boomplaats, in 1848, British troops were for a third time used for Griqua purposes . . . . . Instead of applying a sweeping declaration of sovereignty, Griqua authority was cobbled-up, and complications naturally ensued. The battle of Boomplaats in 1848 was followed by the exodus in 1862, and, in still more recent times, bv a dispute as to ownership of the Diamond Fields, settled by a payment of £90,000 to the Free State. The Maitland Treaty was the first of the contrivances above mentioned. By it the territory of Kok was divided into alienable and inalienable. Purchasers in the latter being Boers, were considered to have a 40 years' lease, and all lessees were bound to quit as their terms expired. In the former, Boers held tenure under Kok, who received half of the quitrents, Government defraying expenses of Resident, etc., with remainder. Under the Smith Treaty Kok gave up his share of quitrents for £300 per annum in perpetuity, £200 for himself and £100 for his people, in consideration of "the lands they have let," some 40 years' leases in the alienable territory being thus converted into leases in perpetuity or ownership; (2) lessees in the inalienable territory, being British subjects, to retire with expiring of lease, having been paid value of improvements, which failing, lease to continue until an equivalent accumulation in rental; (3) British Resident, Kok's Secretary, and an emigrant farmer to make valuation, vote of majority being decisive. The Kaptyn was wont plaintively to say that Sir Harry, whose bark was ever worse than his bite, gave him the option of signing this treaty or being "hung from the *unplaned* beam of a Boer's house," yet the document winds up with this remarkable postscript:—"Kaptyn Adam Kok begs to add the arrangement as to houses and leases in the inalienable territory is entirely his own." An arrangement of this sort could have but one result in the unchangeable order of nature, yet the crisis was precipitated by the convention with the Free State, an article in which constituted Europeans, residents of six months north of the Orange River, subjects of the Republic. West Griqualand was vested in chief and state; but the Philipolis country, being given out in individual titles, soon slipped from Griqua grasp. Piet Draai, whose memory extends over fifty years, says that many sold from "pure naughtiness." Eviction of the Griqua Government, if not of the people, therefore became yearly more imperative. Application of native laws to Europeans, a difficult matter where few are concerned, is indefinitely aggravated when the few have become many, with separate jurisdiction and individual holdings instead of a feeble right to wander over tribal property. Withdrawal of sovereignty left the Griquas in presence of more difficulties than ever. Even Sir George Clerk realized this, and therefore proposed that "all those farms that were in the occupation of Boers should be sold for prices varying from 500 to 1,500 rix-dollars," but Kok refusing to consent, the departure of the Royal Commissioner found him still in a dilemma. Sales naturally multiplied, and on 31st January, 1857, under the article above mentioned, the Free State divided the whole of the territory, not excluding Philipolis itself, into field-cornetcies, and proclaimed every white inhabitant thereof a subject of the Republic. A seizure of Griquas on their farms, and their imprisonment in Free State gaols, followed; and when transfers of Griqua farms began to be effected at Fauresmith, Kok felt that he must clear out or come to blows. Electing for the former, with Sir George Grey's approval, he led over a hundred pioneers into Nomansland, about which he seems to have been enlightened by Smith Pommer. This was early in 1859. Skirting the present site of Dordrecht, heading the Tsomo and Gatberg, they debouched into the country when it was looking its greenest. Game was abundant, and even lions, which infested the Ingele and Umzimvubu, were killed. Naturally delighted with everything they saw and picturing to themselves unlimited supplies of coffee and sugar, to be raised in this land of promise, they returned direct over the Drakensberg. Widening a footpath as they went along, the summit was reached at Ongeluks Nek, so called in commemoration of the death of one who was killed while drawing a gun from a wagon. The descending ridge being too narrow for vehicles, the summit was followed for several miles, and then, with a sweep westward, the descent began. Though retarded by reims and treble lockings the downward journey was accomplished only too quickly. It was a safer but more tedious and laborious process to cross the kloofs and spurs near the Orange River. But Morosi's kraal once passed, Hanglip soon rose to view; then Smithfield; and last of all, Philipolis itself was reached in safety. Making his report in January, 1860, the people stimulated by an imagination of the castle building sort, voted heartily for a "trek."

The winter of that year saw the formation of a camp at Hanglip, where an iron church was erected, and all the people assembled by the end of 1862. The last year was a memorable year for drought. Stock perished on every side. The very air was tainted because numberless vultures could not devour the carrion. Griquas were particularly unfortunate. Losses of 500 sheep were common, owners of a thousand lost 900, and others, 1,000, 1,200, and 1,500. Milch cows, upon which rich and poor alike depended, either died or were stolen by Basutos. Leaving Hanglip, the ascent began, women and children, with those of sterner stuff, enduring the hardships of the mountain pass. "Compensatie" is a word printed large in the Griqua dictionary; it would poll more votes than any other in the language; and in the new sphere, once more at its greenest, Griquas found compensation for the tawny regions left behind. But the old ill soon found them out, because the old causes, with new ones super-added, were at work. The country was less pastoral than Philipolis, while stock had to become accustomed to the veld. The internal were worse than the external troubles, and thus it came to pass that many who were "wealthiest at Philipolis are poorest now." First called Bastards, and their country Bastardland, the run of Griquas resemble their Hottentot mothers in colour, face and hair, rather than the European fathers whose name they bear. The name "Griqua" was assumed in 1813, when "Bastard" was used to distinguish "those whose physiological features for several generations partook more of the white Boer than of the coloured mother; and they inherited a lighter colour, cheek bones more depressed, a more respectable nose, and long or curly hair, and were therefore not considered of the aristocracy, even though in some cases wealthier." Their political and material ups-and-downs have been numerous. Speaking of the deplorable condition of the *West* Griqualand people, a writer traces it to:— (1) Difficulty of pastoral supervision over a people scattered by the water conditions of a dry country; (2) melting away of race; (3) being pastoral like Arabs, not agricultural like Bechuanas; (4) tribal holdings; (5) progressive desiccation; (6) lungsickness; (7) improvidence, indolence, pride, ignorance and carelessness—from all which it is clear the people are "as alike as two peas." Klaarwater, which irrigated miles of country in 1813, has now retired into a hole, about nine feet deep, from which a few wretched families get water barely sufficient for household purposes. About the time of the exodus, however, circumstances seem to have been fairly prosperous with the Griquas of Philipolis. It is said that, having titles, substantial cottages and outbuildings had been erected; orchards were well stocked with fruit trees; on most farms were to be found good stone walls and dams, together with troops of horses, ranging from 20 to 100, and cattle in equal proportion; while many a man brought 10, 15, 20, and even 25 bales of fine wool to market. They contributed between £500 and £600 to the support of religion and education. . . . . Ever eager for present good, Griquas now desire to capitalize the £300 paid under the Smith Treaty; and to arrange for its equitable apportionment will be a work of some difficulty. As a matter of course the capitalized £100 will go to those individuals who relinquish certain annual rights; but what about the £200 given to Kok in lieu of quitrent, he being the

Griqua Government, and quitrents universally belonging to the Treasury? Do his representatives, or the British Government, or the people take that? Say some: The British Government has stepped into the shoes of the Griqua Government with respect to liabilities and assets, and should therefore receive the £200. But *per contra*, whatever the origin of the money, it was never applied to public purposes; it was not even shared with the Raad, but was used by the Kaptyn in promoting his own comfort, and, in the event of capitalization during his lifetime, he, and through him his heirs, would probably have enjoyed the whole benefit. Had Kok been deposed and a successor elected, it is dubious if the destination of the annual payment would have been altered. On the other hand, it may be said that Kok's pocket and the Treasury were one and the same thing, to which he went for money equally for public and for domestic purposes. These are some of the considerations that will arise in the event of the people making a claim, and that claim being referred for determination on principles of general equity.

REPORT OF SELECT COMMITTEE ON NATIVE AFFAIRS 1873.

Memorandum by Mr. Orpen regarding the state of the following Chiefs and People, viz.:—Lebenya, Zibi, Lehana, Makwai, Lipeane, Ludidi, Silonyana, Umtlontlo, Umditshwa, Damas and Umqikela.

LEBENYA, a chief of the Basuto tribe (son of Moyakisani) of the Monaheng clan, of which Motlumi, a former chief, was the head. This Motlumi has the reputation of having been a chief of supernatural sagacity and great kindness, and he became the paramount chief of the different clans of the Basutos before they were broken up by devastating wars originating during the last half century in the new despotic military system and conquest of the Zooloo tribe under Zahenzenga-kona, and his sons Chaka and Dingaan successively. The mantle of Motlumi was believed to have descended with increased power upon his disciple Moshesh, who held out alone against the successive floods of the invasion and collected the clans under his paramount chieftain-ship. But the Monaheng clan were never satisfied altogether with becoming subordinate, and there has always been more or less of a feud between them, which Moshesh could never thoroughly heal, and his sons rather provoked sometimes. Lebenya always bore a dis-tinguished good character on the border of the Sovereignty, the Free State, and the Colony, restraining and punishing thefts while they raged all about him during the disturbances which existed for many years in that part of the country. His conduct was so marked that immediately after the first war between the Free State and Basutos, and although he had loyally fought for his own chief, the Free State, Frontier farmers, and field-cornets, notwithstanding the bitterness of recent war, spoke so highly of him to Sir George Grey, when he was mediating and laying down a new boundary, and this was so corrobo-rated by the report of the Frontier officers of this Colony, that Sir George Grey made him a present publicly of a valuable fowling-piece in token of his regard. He was one of those who after that war (in which the Free State had had the worst, and had called for Sir George Grey's intercession), was the strongest with old Moshesh in desiring and petitioning that the Basutos should be accepted again as Her Majesty's subjects, as I led them to do. He always considered himself a British subject abandoned, and so he was; he had been naturalized by agreement and proclamation, he was abandoned by proclamation, but could never be denaturalized. During the next war his position became untenable, and he considered his clan selfishly abandoned by the others, and he took refuge in the crowded Native Reserve in Aliwal North. The superintendent, during the short interval of peace which followed, obtained leave from Sir Philip Wodehouse for Lebenya to go to occupy a part of the territory ceded to Her Majesty's Govern-ment by Faku, not far from my residence, a day's ride. He went there then as a British subject, as he is, and to British territory. He was still tolerably well off; he and his people plough and sow, and have wagons and oxen, and he and a great part of them wear European clothing. He first took down two thousand head of cattle over the Drakensberg; the path passes through my farm, and I can see the top of the pass through my windows. When he got over the pass he left the cattle in charge of thirteen of his people, sent some on with his written authority to the neighbouring Umpondomisi chiefs, and returned to attend Circuit Court at Burghersdorp, to which he was summoned as a witness. After he had left, a war party from the Umpondomise chief Umtlontlo came up towards his people. They called out that they were people with a Government pass which had been sent to the chiefs—(I believe it had not reached Umtlontlo)—and one of Lebenya's men went over to speak to them. They called for the others, and all went but one—Lebenya's brother among the rest. The one who stayed mistrusted Umtlontlo's men, and ensconced himself with his gun in a cave. After sitting together for some time, Umtlontlo's men suddenly fell upon Lebenya's, and murdered them all, and took the two thousand head of cattle. Lebenya never got any redress; of course he reported it, but it never seems to have struck Government that it had any duty towards these its subjects on this its territory. Some years afterwards, in 1869, Sir Philip Wodehouse passed down through that part of the country, and told Lebenya a certain part of it would be allotted jointly to him and the chief Zibi who accompanied His Excellency. It was at that time Sir Philip Wodehouse said in his opening speech that there was so much reason to regard with satisfaction the political position "we" held there, and that "we" had "undisputed authority," and he had "located" Basutos, Fingoes, etc., there. Lebenya and his people are British subjects by the first proclamation of the Orange River Sovereignty in 1848, and again by the reception of the Basutos by proclamation in 1869.

ZIBI is one of the highest in rank of the chiefs of that Fingo tribe called the Amahlubi, one branch of which is settled in the Colony of Natal, where they are known under the general name of Zooloo. He lived for some twenty years in the Wittebergen Native Reserve in the Aliwal North district, and was always well conducted. He wears European clothes, reads and writes and is baptized, and he and his people have wagons, ploughs, etc. The Reserve being very crowded, Sir Philip Wodehouse, in 1869, took him with him towards Adam Kok's, and told him he might occupy a part of the country in common with Lebenya. The Fingoes are, of course, all British subjects, and have fought on our side in all our wars, and they are accustomed to pay taxes.

LEHANA, of the Batlokoa tribe, is the eldest son of the late chief Sikonyela, but not of the chief house—that son is a minor by agreement and proclamation. Sikonyela was made a British subject with his people when the "Sovereignty" was proclaimed over the Orange River. Sikonyela and the Batlokoas were made use of by officers of Government against the Basutos; the one set upon the other for ulterior objects, while all of them together were British subjects, and instead of superiorising and controlling them from within, they were ruled by main force from without in utter blindness as to the real state of affairs among them, and to our and their great misfortune. The Batlokoa British subjects lost their country in consequence, and moved into the Colony before the abandonment of the Sovereignty, and most of them went into service, but their chiefs were located in the Native Reserve in the district of Aliwal North. When their people returned from service with stock, the Reserve was too crowded for them, and they were sent to occupy their present position. There is some question as to whether they did not obtain their first title to occupy through Nehemiah Moshesh, and in territory ceded by Faku to Moshesh; but it is immaterial, as either way it became British territory through the Basuto's cession to us, or Faku's cession to us. There was no difficulty in governing the Batlokoas in the Colony; they ploughed and sowed, and went out to work, and brought home the proceeds of their labour, and paid taxes like others. The chiefs are people who wear European clothes, and they have their wagons, oxen, etc.

These three, Lebenya, Lehana, and Zibi, had latterly had some fighting among themselves just before the Commission went to that part and arranged their disputes and censured them for their misbehaviour, and they, in the submissive way these people have, acknowledged the censure was just, and so, no doubt, it was; but at the same time they said that the only way to prevent such things was to give them a magistrate and govern them, and they would be perfectly willing to be taxed to support him. That was their mild way of suggesting that this lawlessness was the simple result of want of law, and it implies that the Government is primarily to blame for not giving them law which is their due. Now, I knew these men intimately, and I can throw the full deserved amount of blame more unreservedly upon the Government than they dare do, and tell what they explain to me as to their position, and how it is difficult for them to keep out of these hostilities. With regard to Lebenya, it will be remembered the position in which he immediately found himself upon entering that country, that British territory in which he, a British subject, was plundered, and his brethren and men murdered. He told me he was in consequence necessitated to seek alliances to protect himself. Lehana told me the same thing—that Government neglected its territory and left it lawless, and those who would gladly have rested and been at peace, were forced to alliances with one or other of the stronger tribes who were fighting with each other in order to obtain that protection which their Government denied them; and these alliances were, of course, reciprocal, and involved them in these feuds. Zibi, I know, found his special alliance in the same way, and it unfortunately happened, as I have heard, that the tract of country allotted to him and Lebenya, was given in common, and not divided. It is little to be wondered at that they should have differences, thrown thus together to scramble for the best localities, with no law or authority to mediate between them. I heard, too, that Zibi had driven Lebenya's people by force with armed parties from lands they at first cultivated. I am in doubt whether the Commission went as far back as this, or were able to do so in discussing the conduct of Lebenya, who, I see, they censured more leniently than Lehana. I am not, however, concerned to exculpate Lebenya. I am only concerned to know that a man, who had maintained a good character under very great misrule in Basutoland, should at last, under an abominable utter refusal of all rule or obligations of Sovereignty on the part of our Government, have misbehaved himself and incurred the censure of the Commission; and that those who might have been good friends under any good direction and control, had been involved in hostility with each other. The case of these three clans is illustrative of the whole state of affairs in that wretched possession of Her Majesty's Government. It nearly comes to this, that every clan has an enemy on each side, and an ally beyond the enemy, and every hostility involves a number of other hostilities; and the people everywhere concentrated and on the qui vive, and in alarm, if not in war. It is a constant state of misery; and yet these very divisions show how easy it would be to rule it if they are but understood; and they would be most relieved and grateful if Government did its duty, and intervened between them all. They would subside into peace and industry immediately, as the natives have done everywhere else where Government has introduced its authority among them. I ride over a mountain at one side of my farm, and I look down on the "Native Reserve," a small tract of country, crowded with 20,000 inhabitants, and covered with cornfields, and only too much stock to live there. That is the home of our labourers, to which they return, and there their stock die out from overcrowding, and they become discouraged from going out to earn more. I go over a mountain on the other side of the valley, and I see one of the fairest prospects in the world—a magnificent wide country spread out like a map below me, and but little stock, and the people huddled together for defence; and they are the very same people—the same families. It was thought the "Reserve" would almost empty itself into this country; but, as the superintendent has expressed it, they prefer being crowded and cramped under Government to being crushed beyond its rule, and that in country that is British territory, which we are bound to govern, and could govern with ease, and at no expense to ourselves, if we only sent a few magistrates who could adjudicate between the people.

LUDIDI is a Fingo chief, a relative of Zibi's. He, and the Amabaca, under Silonyana, alias Makaula, the son of the late Ncapai, have assisted us in every war since 1836. There are a number of the Amabaca also under Adam Kok.

MAKWAAI is Moshesh's first cousin of the elder branch. His father Dibe, was chief of the clan, but was a churl, and his people deposed him in favour of Moshesh's father. He is an active, Arab-featured man, much thought of in the tribe, and a well-conducted chief, civilized in appearance, and wearing European clothing. In Basutoland, his clean European house was always open to visitors, and his English-speaking wife used to serve nice European food for them on a clean tablecloth, and treat them hospitably. He lost his country in the war with the Free State, and went down into the country between the Kenegha and the Umzimvooboo, which the Basutos hold to be part of Basutoland, obtained from Faku by concession to them, and made over to Government by the cession of Basutoland to Her Majesty, but which Government holds to be part of the country obtained directly from Faku by cession to Government. Sir Philip Wodehouse seeing his hands tied, and his inability to establish Government authority there, adopted the expedient of placing Makwaai and the whole territory between the Umzimvooboo and the Kenegha under Adam Kok's protection and authority, retaining the Basutos' right of residence, but making them liable to hut-tax. This they have since paid always to Adam Kok's Government. The ground in question was made over to Adam Kok conditionally on a cession, not afterwards carried out, to the Natal Government, and he was eventually allowed to retain "possession" of it. Being Basutos, Makwaai's people are British subjects. The Baphuti clan of Basutos, chief Lipeani, the original settlers in Basutoland, in the migration of those tribes some generations ago southward, reside lower down to the west of the Umzimvooboo, and pay taxes to the Griquas. They are British subjects. Makwaai and they have never made any disturbances, but have been "commandeered" by Adam Kok against others.

All the foregoing clans are easily managed people.

The UMPONDOMISI split clan under Umtlontlo and Umditshwa, always at feud with each other and all round, might be somewhat more difficult to keep in order; but they have both of them, I believe, now asked again to be received as British subjects like the others. I know Umtlontlo has, and I have not the slightest doubt they could be easily managed, if they saw Government picking up the reins and establishing its authority around them. They are, after all, only a small clan.

With regard to the Basutos and Fingos, they are undoubtedly British subjects, naturalized by formal proclamation and mutual agreement. No lawyer will dispute that, or say that they can be denaturalized; and with regard to the Umpondomisi and Amabaca clans, I can really see no proper difference in their case. They and their country were made over by their paramount chief to Her Majesty, and the concession is accepted and "maintained," and they asked at the time, and they ask still, to have the prerogatives and duties of the Sovereignty thus accepted over them exercised for their benefit. I do not see what difference a formal proclamation in a Government Gazette would make. The fact was proclaimed to them long since, and they are entitled to claim the exercise of Sovereignty for their protection individually and collectively against each other and all others. They have asked it for years in vain, and I hold that the expression of their wish has the force of a formal and legal demand that the correlative duties of Sovereignty shall be exercised. They have not the self-assertion and knowledge of law to put it in this way, and it is time for an advocate to take up their case.

Damas is the eldest son, but not the heir, of Faku, late chief of the Amapondo, and not far from independent of his young brother of the chief house.

Umqikela is the younger brother, but of the chief house, and the successor of Faku. I have proved our protectorate alliance over the Amapondo elsewhere, and their good service to Government, whatever their faults may be. That protectorate alliance imposes a duty upon Government to do what it can to prevent the feuds and hostilities which prevail among them, and particularly that with the Amaxesibe which appears now to be rather indirectly and unintendedly fermented through our own influence, and that with Umtlontlo within the country ceded to us. But Government has long since removed the British residency from among them, and rendered mediation utterly impracticable. Without a resident representative to apply our influence, all attempts to bring it to bear are worse than useless. They come too late, and they come blindly. I would point out to the Committee the expressions of the Amapondo themselves in the minutes of their meeting, to show how they acknowledge, too, a paramount Sovereignty of Government—"the helper," "the giver and ruler of all," who "gave them" their land, from whom they hold their "title" to their land. This is a real feeling, and one which should be cultivated, and could be brought to grow more and more by proper influence systematically and justly exerted. I think Government officers ought to be appointed to guide this very numerous and powerful tribe by Government influence. It is like having the very rudder of Kafirland without a steersman, to have left this so long not done.

The GRIQUAS, under Adam Kok, in the country ceded to Government by Faku, on condition of Her Majesty's governing it, are now but few in number, I believe only a few hundred altogether, the rest having scattered over the Colony, Natal, the Free State, and independent Namaqualand. But by the authority derived from our Government, and the arms, cannon, and ammunition with which we have furnished them, they were able, immediately on their arrival in the country they now occupy, to bring into subordination and impose taxes upon the natives already occupying it, who even then far outnumbered them, and they have since added greatly to the number of the subordinates, and Sir Philip Wodehouse, by extending their boundary to the Kenegha, added still more natives to their rule, and made them also subject to taxes to the Griquas.

As will be seen, Adam Kok was allowed to settle in British territory on the condition dated 1st August, 1860, that they should go as British subjects. This was previous to Sir George Grey's receiving a protest, dated 25th December, 1860, from Faku, against Adam Kok's emigration, and previous to Faku's eventually agreeing in March, 1861, to the proposal that Adam Kok should go there subject to Her Majesty's rule, which further determined the question of their going to occupy country ceded to us as British territory, and that they thereby became British subjects. He has, however, been left almost independent, and Sir Philip alludes to his delegated authority, "as so far as it is recognized by us," and speaks of his holding the country "under the High Commissioner" (see mem. on the Amapondo).

Adam Kok received £100 per annum from the Colonial revenue, and £300 per annum from the Imperial revenue, "in perpetuity," in terms of treaty 24th January, 1848, which Sir G. Clerk declared void, and Sir G. Grey forced the Imperial Government so far to recognize, and when he refused to call upon the Colony to pay that amount.

GATBERG PEOPLE.—A number of well-to-do men of colour, and some English, Dutch, and German farmers, Fingos, Basutos, etc.

DATES OF ANNEXATION TO THE COLONY OF THE CAPE OF GOOD HOPE OF THE SEVERAL DIVISIONS COMPRISING THE TRANSKEIAN TERRITORIES.

1. *The Transkei,*—that is "the country between the Bashee and the Kei," annexed by Act 38 of 1877.

2. *East Griqualand,*—that is "the country situated between the Umtata and Umzimkulu, commonly known as 'Nomansland'" (excluding the Xesibe country and the Rode Valley) annexed by Act No. 38 of 1877.

3. *Port St. John's,*—that is "the Port and tidal estuary of the St John's river in South Africa and certain lands on the banks of the said river." Handed over to the Cape Government by the Pondo chief Mqikela in consideration of the payment to him of a subsidy of £200 per annum. Annexed by Act No. 35 of 1884.

4. *Tembuland*—(Tembuland, Emigrant Tembuland, Gcalekaland, and Bomvanaland. Annexed by Act No. 3 of 1885.)

5. *The Xesibe Country,*—the present District of Mount Ayliff excluding the Rode Valley. Purchased from the Pondo nation on the 9th of December 1886 for £1,000. Annexed by Act No. 37 of 1886.

6. *The Rode Valley,*—"the country situated between the districts of Mount Ayliff and Mount Frere." Purchased from the Pondo nation for £600 on the 9th of December 1886. Annexed by Act No. 45 of 1886·

7. *Pondoland,*—"comprising the territories of East and West Pondoland." Annexed by Act No 5 of 1894.